Books by Art Linkletter

PEOPLE ARE FUNNY

KIDS SAY THE DARNDEST THINGS

THE SECRET WORLD OF KIDS

CONFESSIONS OF A HAPPY MAN

KIDS STILL SAY THE DARNDEST THINGS

KIDS SURE RITE FUNNY

A CHILD'S GARDEN OF MISINFORMATION

OOPS!

OOPS!
Or, Life's Awful Moments

Oops!

OR,

LIFE'S AWFUL MOMENTS

by Art Linkletter

DOUBLEDAY & COMPANY, INC., GARDEN CITY, NEW YORK

1967

Illustrated by Phil Interlandi

FIRST EDITION

LIBRARY OF CONGRESS CATALOG CARD NUMBER 66-24321

PRINTED IN THE UNITED STATES OF AMERICA

CONTENTS

INTRODUCTION *Embarrassing Moments Come in a Thousand Shades* ix

1 *"Oh, No!"* 1

2 *"My Mommy Says"* 15

3 *Blushers at Work* 39

4 *Pants à Go-go* 55

5 *Havoc for Housewives* 65

6 *Boo-boos and Dum-dums* 83

7 *"Oops!"* 103

8 *Highway Hangups* 121

9 *The Name Game* 129

10 *"Passports, Please"* 141

INTRODUCTION

Embarrassing Moments Come in a Thousand Shades

Have you ever tried to put your best foot forward and found it wedged firmly in your mouth? Or done your utmost to make a big impression on some very important person and come off looking like Boob McNutt? Chances are you have, because the road of life is strewn with the banana peels of embarrassment.

I've spent a career having fun with guests on my television and radio shows, and I've found that people are never funnier than when they're upended by an embarrassing moment and dropped flat on their dignities. Nothing is more hilarious than any one of us human beings caught off guard, and that's why no gag writer could possibly invent zanier stories than the ones you will find in this book.

Embarrassing moments come in a thousand shades, from the delicate pink of a shy maiden's cheek to the flaming crimson of a matron whose new minister came calling and walked in on her in the bathtub.

Some embarrassing moments sound like they're straight out of an old Mack Sennett comedy. A contractor does a beautiful job of wrecking an old home and then learns he's gone to the wrong address. A man sneezes during a badminton game—and his false teeth go sailing across the net like a birdie. A lady does a jackknife into the pool while her bathing suit does a swan in a separate direction, leaving her blushing all over. Hundreds of people in a cathedral look up from their prayer books as a little boy hears the chimes of Mass and happily shouts, "Avon calling!"

Although you readers know me for my books on children, such as *Kids Say the Darndest Things* and its sequels, I have long had the urge to write this particular book about the comedy of the adult world in real-life situations. I'm grateful to hundreds of my television and radio listeners who sent me their own most embarrassing moments, after I made an appeal for personal stories on my "House Party" show on CBS-TV.

Some of my favorite stories of embarrassing situations have become classics, such as the one about the young lady who had hay fever. Before going to a formal dinner party, she stuffed some handkerchiefs down her bosom just in case she began sneezing. Sure enough, she did. By the time dessert arrived, she was very intent on fumbling about in her bodice, fishing for another handkerchief. Looking up for an instant, she was terribly flustered to see that all eyes were upon her, so she blurted out, "Well, I know I had *two* when I came in."

Another classic blooper involved a wealthy matron who called the hospital to ask about the condition of her butler. The nurse who answered said, "He's very sick. Are you his wife?" "Certainly not," said the matron. "I'm his mistress."

One of America's greatest orators was William Jennings Bryan, who ran for President against William F. McKinley. It was during that campaign that the silver-tongued Bryan made an inspiring speech and in a sentimental vein concluded, "Tonight my dear wife is sleeping in a little inn, down by the railroad tracks. But come November, she'll be sleeping in the White House!" A man in the audience yelled out, "And if she is, she'll be sleeping with McKinley!"

One of our modern statesmen, Senator Robert F. "Bobby" Kennedy, was the innocent victim of a diplomatic blooper in the midst of his otherwise triumphant tour of Africa. As he got off his plane in Nairobi to be greeted by Kenya's president, Tom Mboya, Kennedy was surrounded by a cheering throng of Africans. Jauntily he gave his well-wishers a "thumbs-up" signal—and the crowd gasped in dismay. In much of the world, thumbs-up means OK—but not in Nairobi. Here the thumbs-up signal had been used as a campaign symbol by the opposition Communist Party!

Naturally I've had my share of embarrassing moments, too, including one I'll never forget that happened on my "People Are Funny" show. After years of playing atrocious tricks on contestants, we decided to have some fun at my expense, to prove that I could take it, too. So we set up a two-minute auction, offering the person in the studio audience who contributed the most money to charity the surprising chance to come on stage and hit me with a chocolate cream pie. The bidding began, and it was almost frightening the way it reached two hundred dollars in less than a minute! Then the high bidder came up the aisle—a sweet little old gray-haired, grandmotherly-looking lady. She wrote out her personal check for the two hundred dollars, picked up the pie—but unlike most amateurs, she didn't just give it a dab toward me. She sent it off with the full, flat-out treatment. Not only did she smash it completely across my face, but as she hit me she turned it clockwise—which put the meringue under my eyelids! It was a real corkscrew smash, in the best Soupy Sales tradition. I can still taste it. And the end of this story is not yet, because the following week the check came back marked "maker unknown." I'd been had! So the next time you see me peering intently at the faces in an audience, you will know that I am really looking to find a certain little old lady.

As Mark Twain once observed, "Man is the Only Animal that blushes. Or needs to." Of course the great humorist was wagging his finger at us all for the kind of wrongdoing that brings forth a blush of shame. But there are many more kinds of blushes that are kindled by situations where we haven't done anything shameful—merely awkward, foolish, absurd . . . and funny! And so I say, quite unblushingly, that this is a book to laugh by. Don't be surprised if a page here and there suddenly becomes a mirror and you find yourself staring up, red-faced, in a situation that once happened to you. Life leaves us all looking a little ridiculous at times, so we might as well relax and enjoy it when the laugh is on us. With these words, I invite you to read on. The first blush is on me!

OOPS!

Or, Life's Awful Moments

1

"Oh, No!"

Like a balloon blowing up in your face, embarrassing moments are always surprising and unexpected. One moment you're poised and confident, feeling good and even proud of yourself. The next instant you're trapped in some dreadful situation, looking foolish and stripped of all your dignity. It's bad enough when only one person sees you at this terrible moment—but think how it feels when a whole gallery is looking on!

I'll never forget the first time I was invited to go riding with the Rancheros Vistadores, a group of California VIPs who go horseback riding together on annual camp-outs. As a newcomer I was persuaded to volunteer for the highlight of the traditional rodeo, a wild-cow-milking contest. I was given a partner, an amateur like myself, who had a rope around the cow's neck as it came roaring out of the chute. We were supposed to haul it across a white line fifteen yards in front of the chute. Then while my partner held the cow, I was to milk it into a pop bottle.

The whole camp was watching as I lined up with my partner, pop bottle in hand. I was fairly confident, since I had asked cowboy star Monty Montana earlier for tips on what to do. He had told me, "No matter how that cow is bucking, remember it's not a real *wild* cow. It's been milked before. So the minute you ram your head right into its flank, it'll stop bucking." Well, I got out there and couldn't believe it. This animal was bucking up and down like crazy. But I followed directions and rammed my head into its side, and it did seem to hesitate for an instant. I had my bottle all ready in my left hand, so I reached under with the other. Just as I did, I took a precautionary look. What was this? No faucets! They'd sent out a bull! Later on we did get a chance at a regular cow—faucets and all—and won the contest.

Here's one that happened in a crowded elevator:

A young executive said hello to one of the company secretaries and then commented admiringly about a bracelet she wore that featured exotic charms. She replied, "Isn't it gorgeous? I've been collecting these for years."

Just then the elevator stopped at the girl's floor and as she stepped out she turned and said, "Someday, when you have time, I'll show you all my charms." Then the elevator door closed, leaving the young man with a very curious and interested group of fellow passengers.

A Los Angeles woman has vivid memories of the night she appeared in a Little Theater group play, in a costume that included a string of heavy glass beads. In the middle of a tense scene, the string broke—and with every step she took, a bead would work its way down under her costume with a loud "plop" as it hit the stage. Plop, plop went the beads as the audience roared. Finally she couldn't ignore the obvious any longer, and fled into the wings.

*   *   *   *

Back in the days of Prohibition a Michigan lady visited her sister in Canada and decided to smuggle some whisky back over the border. She poured it carefully into a flat bottle, tied it in a sack, and concealed it inside her brassiere. She got past the border inspector with no trouble, but as soon as she got on a streetcar in Detroit the cork worked loose and the bottle's pungent contents gurgled into her lap. As everyone began to sniff and stare, she looked grimly ahead, her jaw locked in an innocent expression. Finally her stop came and as she got up to leave, the passengers began to sing "Show Me the Way to Go Home."

A good friend of mine, Ray Stark, is a prominent Hollywood producer. While filming in England, he and his wife attended a rather stuffy and terribly formal reception given by nobility in a big castle. As the Starks entered an imposing reception hall, a man in servant's livery approached them and inquired politely, "And what is yours?" Mistaking him for a waiter, Ray said, "Two Bloody Marys." The man turned, walked to the head of the stairs, and announced to the crowd: "Mr. and Mrs. Bloody Mary."

A lady stopping off at a restaurant noticed that a gentleman at a nearby table had left a huge lamb chop behind on his plate. Thinking it would be a tasty treat for her two hungry dogs waiting in the car, she grabbed it. She was just rolling her juicy prize up in a napkin to stuff it in her purse when a waitress tapped her on the shoulder and said, "The gentleman who was eating at that table just stepped away for a telephone call."

A high school girl was high-stepping along in her majorette costume in the big town parade. She'd gone about a block when a lady darted out of the crowd, pulled the startled girl to one side, and whispered something that ended that

particular majorette's prancing for the day. "My dear girl," the lady said, "you forgot to wear your tights."

Another young lady was learning to water-ski. Like many a beginner, she kept tumbling back into the water. At last she succeeded in struggling upright and went swooshing triumphantly along, having an exhilarating time. Several boats came by with people waving, and she proudly waved back. Finally one boat circled very close and the passengers pointed insistently down at her skis. She looked—and there around her ankles was her entire bathing suit.

*   *   *   *

A listener of mine in Hollywood sent in this one, and I'll let him tell it in his own way:

"It was around midnight, and raining. I'd been driving all day and was hopelessly lost in the country so I started looking for a place to stay overnight. Just as I was about to give up, I saw a small sign in my headlights—'Sunshine Motel.' I turned off and followed the narrow road to an attractive group of buildings. I woke up the clerk and was assigned a room.

"The next morning I put on my bathrobe and walked down the hall to the shower room. I was in the midst of showering when I heard feminine voices and laughter.

"My shower curtain was pulled open, and there stood a smiling and very shapely young lady. I could see exactly how shapely she was, because I could see all of her shape. She was nude! This was my most embarrassing moment, but it certainly wasn't hers. I had checked into a nudist colony."

Perhaps one of the reasons that I'm so often asked to be master of ceremonies at big formal dinners is because of my irreverent attitude. Frankly, I dislike pretentious affairs and banquets, and all the stuffy rituals that turn normally nice people into posturing mannequins. Even the people who organize such affairs dread the necessary ceremonies, so they invite me to sit at the head table and sprinkle a little salt on the sugary confections of the speakers. The greatest pomposity-popper of us all was Will Rogers, who said that the bigger they are, the more you can poke goose feathers at them. Bob Hope is probably our nimblest feather-poker to-day. In my own smaller way I've kidded everybody in the land, except possibly the President. (To his face.)

*　*　*　*

Recently I was master of ceremonies for one of the most formal dinners ever held in Los Angeles. The churchman who gave the opening invocation kept going for a full ten minutes. It became embarrassing to everyone as he went on and on. Finally he concluded, and I commented that we should all observe yet another moment of silence because a new world's record in being thankful had just been set. I announced that he had even outlasted my father in this department—and my father's saying grace at table was so long that I never had a bite of hot food until I was twenty-one.

*　*　*　*

One of the greatest catastrophes that ever happened to me in public occurred when I was presiding at a very large dinner in a downtown Los Angeles hotel for one of the first coast-to-coast "Emmy" Award programs. Everybody was being so formal and pompous amid the smell of mothballs from rented tuxedos. I was introduced, walked out on stage, and just as I said, "Good evening, ladies and gentlemen," the master light switch exploded and plunged the hall into darkness. Stagehands began running in all directions, knocking the entire Grecian set down. Walls, pillars, and great façades tumbled onto the orchestra. One entire section of strings was knocked out by an enormous pillar. When the lights came on again and order was slowly restored, I stood calmly looking out over the wreckage, and instead of making everyone even more embarrassed by trying to apologize or explain, I said, "For an encore, ladies and gentlemen, we will now set fire to Lucille Ball."

Another dinner at the world-famous Cocoanut Grove in Los Angeles honored the president of a very large university. He was to come to the microphone and pick up an award, then walk over and present it to his wife. He was wired for sound with a small portable short-wave microphone transmitter, wires running down his pants and batteries in his back pocket. This gadgetry was to carry his voice from a microphone in his lapel to a backstage receiver for relaying to the audience through a public address speaker. But as he walked toward his wife, his sending set somehow became a radio receiver, as sometimes can happen. Suddenly over the public address system, straight from the man's back pocket, came a dignified commanding voice, "When you want a *real* fertilizer, get Vigoro!"

There seems to be some kind of law operating which guarantees that the most embarrassing incidents imaginable will happen in front of the maximum number of people. Movie theaters, dance floors, restaurants, and even sports stadiums are frequently the arenas where some poor innocent meets an all-too-public fate.

*   *   *   *

A lady at a movie removed her new false teeth because they were bothering her. Later on the film broke, the lights came on unexpectedly, and she popped her molars back in her mouth. She started to say something to the man sitting next to her when she became aware that he was staring at her in a most curious way. In her haste she had put her teeth in upside down!

*   *   *   *

Another woman followed her husband down the theater aisle, fought her way past knees and over legs, took her seat, reached over, and began digging in and munching on their popcorn. She was halfway through the bag when a meek little man beside her said, "Save some for me, will you, lady?" Her husband was several seats away.

The modern age of electronics caught up with a pair of teen-age girls who double dated some boys at a drive-in movie. During the intermission, while the boys were gone for refreshments, the girls said exactly what they thought of their dates. Imagine what the girls felt like later when the boys returned, showed them a tape recorder hidden under the seat, and proceeded to play back for them every word of their feline gossip.

*   *   *   *

Celebrating a wedding anniversary, a Brooklyn couple went out to dinner and a Broadway play. The wife ate so heartily that when she reached the theater she loosened her wraparound skirt. During intermission she followed her husband out and found she was now the theater's main attraction. She'd left her skirt behind in her seat.

A lady attending a Hollywood Bowl concert by Jascha Heifetz brought along an inflated rubber pillow. It was too high for her, so while Mr. Heifetz was serenading, she decided to soften the pillow by lowering the air pressure.

When she removed the plug, out came one of the loudest Bronx cheers ever heard at a concert. To this day her husband can start a family quarrel simply by saying, "Have I ever told you about the time my wife accompanied Jascha Heifetz?"

It was a museum, of all places, where a New Hampshire lady suffered one of her life's darkest moments. She and her husband were touring the painting gallery when her little boy called her away to see the enormous skeleton of a prehistoric beast. When she returned to the gallery, her husband seemed to be very intent in studying a canvas of a voluptuous nude. She sneaked up behind this avid admirer of the form undraped and murmured, "How would you like to take her to bed with you, kid?" A startled stranger whirled around to face an even more startled woman.

If you've ever watched the mysterious gyrations on teen-age television shows that pass for dancing, you'll enjoy this story from a young lady who writes, "I was standing on the edge of the crowd on the dance floor when a boy came over and started to do the Frug. I joined in and thanked him when it was over. 'I wasn't dancing,' he said. 'I was just trying to get past you to the vending machine.'"

It was "stop the music" time for another woman who was dancing so enthusiastically that her contact lens popped out and went bouncing across the floor. Her husband quick-stepped to the bandleader with a special request—"Stop playing!"—and all the dancers did the crouch until they found the lens.

A dozen young men were standing around in the shower of a certain YMCA where they were accustomed to swimming in the nude. Somebody yelled, "The last one in the pool is a rotten egg." Everybody ran and jumped in—and

then scrambled out again and ran into the locker room. It was "mixed bathing" day!

A coach famous for his super-inspirational pep talks was known as a "locker-room Billy Graham." While visiting a campus with his football team for the first time, he got the boys all fired up in the locker room, pointed to the swinging doors at the far end, and said, "Now, get out there and tear those guys to pieces!" Led by the star quarterback, the team charged through the open doors—straight into a swimming pool. Half the squad was dunked, and the game had to be held up while their uniforms were dried out.

One of the most determined young athletes I've ever
heard of is the hero of this next story:

It was the day of the big high school track meet. Thousands of spectators were in the stands as half a dozen of the
city's finest young men lined up for a sprint. They crouched
down, the official raised the starter's pistol, fired, and away
they raced. "They're off!" cried the announcer on the p.a.
system. And they *were* off—the gym shorts of one of the
competitors. They'd split and fallen under the strain of the
takeoff. Without missing a stride, the boy pulled his jersey
way down with both hands and held it there, speeding along

with the others. Speeding even faster was a titter that raced through the crowd as the spectators realized the boy had lost his pants. He made it all the way to the finish line and got the biggest hand of the day.

One of the most bizarre incidents I've ever had a part in happened at the San Francisco World's Fair in 1939. The Japanese had sent their complete exhibit building direct from Japan, all broken down into numbered pieces like a gigantic jigsaw puzzle. All the pieces were on the deck of a big ship called the *Tatsuta Maru,* and when the ship arrived in the harbor, it was my job to put on a coast-to-coast broadcast about this very important exhibit. The program was on a strict schedule, which included a Buddhist priest saying exactly thirty seconds of incantations over the numerous packing cases on the deck of the ship. All the officials of San Francisco and the Fair were there. The Buddhist priest was a little Japanese fellow who, when he started to pray, shut his eyes tightly, put his fingers together in a clenched position with his elbows out, talking rapidly and pausing only for long intakes of breath. His prayer was apparently quite profound, because all the Japanese present had their heads cast down and their eyes shut, listening intently. But I was watching the stopwatch, dismayed at the way he ran on and on. After the priest prayed three minutes past his allotted time, I saw he was carried away by his own eloquence. I walked up behind him, and when he had finished an especially long sentence and was taking in a long hissing breath, I reached under each elbow—he weighed about eighty pounds and I weighed two hundred—and picked him up and walked away with him. He was still praying, eyes shut, as I walked him out of sight and put him in a cabin. It was a little embarrassing—but "the show has to go on."

2

"My Mommy Says"

Kids are so much fun most of the time that we harassed parents are ready to forgive them almost anything. It's just as well, because sometimes there's quite a lot to forgive. Some of life's most embarrassing moments occur when Junior bursts in on an adult conversation with a little gem about home life that leaves Mother and Dad in shock and the guests giggling audibly, while inaudibly they're making mental notes so they'll have the story right the first time they tell it.

For the past twenty-one years I've been talking to youngsters on my "House Party" program, and from the innocent bombshells they've dropped in that time, I would guess that more families have pulled up stakes and left the old neighborhood as a result than at any time since the Gold Rush.

The other day I asked a young lady of about five to tell us what her mother did for fun.

"She plays golf," she replied, "with a strange man."

"A strange man?" I echoed. "Don't you know who he is?"

She shook her head. "Nobody knows who he is," she said darkly.

"Any other news?" I thought I had better change the subject.

"Well," she said, "Mama's going to have a baby but no one knows why."

Whereupon the studio audience fell into the aisles, and somewhere a perfectly respectable housewife—who no doubt had been taking some innocent lessons from a golf pro—wished she could go bury herself in a sand trap.

A few days later I tried the same question on a young man of seven. "What does your dad do for fun?" I asked him, while millions watched and listened.

"Well," he said a bit sadly, "he used to like hunting and fishing, but now he's just interested in indoor sports."

"What sort of indoor sports?" I inquired.

"I don't know," he said. "He always locks the door."

The question "What do your parents do for fun?" is a gimmick designed to unlock family secrets, and the more unexpected the revelation, the more delighted the audience reaction. One youngster, I remember, confided that his father was a psychiatrist.

"And what does he do for fun?" I asked, braced for anything.

"He reads comics in the bathtub when he's using Mama's bubble bath powder."

And somewhere out in the listening audience, a father-psychiatrist, who had been a proud parent just a moment before, was no doubt dialing a psychiatrist *he* knew to inquire about a head-shrinking session.

But for sheer volume of laughs you can't beat the slightly ribald statement delivered with an air of poker-faced innocence. I asked a young man, aged about six, what his daddy did for fun.

"He sleeps out on the porch," he said.

"Why is that?" I wanted to know.

"Because Mama keeps thrashing around in bed all night and he can't have any fun there at all!"

Occasionally I receive a critical letter from a listener who objects to questions that sometimes lead to these double entendres. My answer is that in any conversation with a youngster the child himself is completely innocent of any wrongdoing. This is the real fun of a child's double entendre —that it is unintentional and said with no idea that it is either amusing or risqué. What the audience is laughing at is not the child, but me, as the stand-in for the parents whose embarrassment is understood, sympathized with, and thoroughly enjoyed.

These hilariously awkward moments caused by innocent kids are happening constantly to red-faced parents around the country, and not just on my show. One woman whose husband is a salesman told me, "My husband travels a lot, and while he's gone, the children take turns sleeping with me. On one trip the kids acted up, so for punishment they had to sleep in their own beds. When we picked my husband up at the airport, our nine-year-old son shouted, 'No one slept with Mom while you were gone, Dad!'" You can bet that family got out of the airport in a hurry.

A kindergarten teacher was having sharing time with her youngsters, asking them what was going on in their lives at home. A little boy got up and said, "My sister has loose morals." A little questioning developed that what he really meant was that his sister had loose molars.

A five-year-old girl was fascinated by watching workmen repairing the street in front of her home. Her grandmother said to her, "Darling, you shouldn't be out there bothering those workmen." "Oh, that's all right, Grandma," the girl answered. "I'm only intimate with one of them."

As a family was settling down to watch TV recently the six-year-old son said, "Hey, Mother, our teacher is back." His older sister explained that the boy's teacher had just returned from her honeymoon. "That's right," said the boy. "She went to Florida for two weeks." Then he added, "She said she'd had a wonderful time, but I doubt it—she wasn't a bit suntanned."

One of the commonest mistakes that parents make is coaching their children to say some certain thing at a certain time. My favorite story of parental prompting is about the lady who told her son, "We're all going to see Uncle George at the hospital today. If he says, 'I'm not feeling well and I'm very sick,' you should say, 'I hope they pull you through.'" So when they visited the hospital, the uncle told the boy, "I'm lying at death's door"—and the boy said, "I hope they pull you through."

Some of the choice embarrassing moments occur on my show as a result of the "brainwashing" that goes on after a child has been selected by his schoolteacher to be one of my little guests. Most parents are fully aware that kids *do* talk freely to me, and for the few weeks just preceding the average child's appearance on "House Party" he is thoroughly briefed by Mother and Dad about dangerous subjects. He is told not to mention Uncle Harry who drinks, Aunt Martha who ran away with the milkman, or what Daddy says about his boss. By the time the little one gets to my program he has been told what not to say so often that he has it down letter perfect, and when I ask him, "What did your folks tell you *not* to say?" he repeats it without missing a verb.

"And what did *your* mother tell you, young man?" I recently asked a six-year-old.

"Not to announce that she is pregnant!" came back his calm reply.

Over the audience shrieks I finally reassured him that all was well. I said, "Being pregnant is a wonderful thing. Why *not* announce it?"

"Mainly," he struggled manfully to correct things, "because she *ain't*."

Usually the mothers get down to the studio to watch the show, while fathers turn on radios or television sets in their offices or other places of business. I often wonder which place is the worse to be when a child comes out with a choice bit of family gossip. The mothers generally give themselves away by an embarrassed yelp, but the fathers are left in a helpless daze as their business associates and friends pounce on them following an exchange like this:

"What does your daddy do for a living?"

"He makes money downstairs in our basement." (Snickers from the studio audience.)

"How does he make money down there?"

"It's some kind of a machine called Studpoker. Men come in every Monday night from all over the neighborhood."

Sometimes a frantic mother will rush backstage after the show to explain what was said, and attempt to clear the family coat of arms. This happened recently when a charming youngster predicted on the air that when he grew up he would be "A bachelor, like my daddy!" The mother assured me that his daddy was *not* a bachelor, but that he had just graduated from the University of Southern California with a bachelor's degree.

Perhaps one of the most startling confessions in the history of the show occurred when a calm, scientific little girl of seven discussed her medical history.

"Oh, I've been to the hospital lots of times, Mr. Linkletter," she had begun. "I've had my tonsils out. I had my adenoids out. I had the mumps. And, oh, yes, I had something else with a funny name." She paused for one suspenseful moment and then came out with the bombshell. "Oh, yes, I remember. I was circumcised!"

As she sat back smiling blissfully and proudly at having remembered the "correct" medical term, the audience broke up completely, and somewhere in the seventh row I could sense that ushers were fanning a lady guest frantically.

On at least one occasion it took the parents weeks to figure out how the child had gotten the wrong idea about his daddy. Almost a month passed before I received a letter which pieced together a world that had fallen down around the ears of a young married couple after their child had appeared on the show and insisted:

"My daddy steals for a living!"

In spite of my close cross-examination the boy would not be put off. He was sure his daddy stole, and he backed up his claim by assuring me that he had heard his folks talk about it at breakfast.

The final explanation is a classic in revealing the strange and wonderful world the children live in—half fantasy, half reality. It's a place where grownup words are only dimly understood and quite often the logic gets oddly twisted, as well. In this family the father had been stuck with a job he hated. Then, after several years of frustration, he had been transferred to an office position that he loved. Understandably, this was often the subject of breakfast talk. Daddy would slap his knee in joy at the prospect of his new duties and say, "Boy, this new job is just like stealing money." Or occasionally he would come out with, "My work is like having a license to steal!" Naturally, to the ears of a child, this kind of statement made just one kind of sense:

"My daddy steals for a living!"

By now the fathers of America should have learned it's risky to call in their friends to watch and listen while their pride and joy tells all on my program. Sheepish letters have confessed to me that pandemonium broke loose in all kinds of business establishments following the candid revelations of youngsters.

The board of directors of Sunkist Orange Growers Association once recessed while the son of the chairman "starred" on "House Party." When I asked him what his daddy did, the youngster proudly announced, "He picks oranges and sometimes they even let him drive the truck."

The police force of a southern California community gathered one day to watch the child of one of their officers tell us that "My daddy is brave and tough. He arrests robbers and burglars and crooks and he has a big black gun."

"Doesn't your mother worry about your daddy getting hurt in a dangerous kind of job like that?" I asked.

"Oh, no," he joyfully explained. "She thinks it's a wonderful job. Almost every week he brings home wristwatches and earrings and all kinds of jewelry!"

I've often wondered about the *next* assignment of that particular father.

The son of a prominent football coach repeated his father's philosophy:

"My daddy thinks most of his players are big dumb jerks.

He says the only position most of them have enough brains to play is bent over!"

And I wonder what a major motion-picture studio executive group must have thought when the son of one of their top writers explained how movies are made:

"My daddy writes a wonderful story, and then those dumb producers ruin it."

Even I don't emerge entirely unscathed from the burp-gun approach of the deadly small fry. The son of one of my cameramen recently said, "My daddy likes this job working on your show, but he says you're sure stingy with a buck!"

I'll never know the *real* lowdown on a conversation I had with a boy whose father worked in a big downtown Los Angeles hotel. It went like this:

"My daddy has a funny kind of a job at a hotel."

"What do you mean 'funny' job?" I probed.

"Well, he's sort of in charge of horse racing!"

"Maybe we'd better change the subject," I interjected quickly as the full import of his remark began to sink in on a snickering audience. "What would *you* like to be when you grow up?"

"I'd like to be a bookkeeper like my father."

There was also a young man who wanted to be a cat when he grew up.

"A cat?" I echoed. "What kind of cat?"

"A tomcat," he said promptly.

"Why a tomcat?" I asked.

"I don't know," he said wistfully, "but that's what my dad says *he'd* like to be!"

Occasionally a youngster balks at talking about his father's job. One young man flatly told me that his dad had clearly instructed him not to tell what he did.

"Why not?" I urged.

"Because it's a kind of a funny word."

"Well, suppose you just try it out on me and see if I think it's funny?"

"All right," he said hesitantly. "He's a stupidvisor."

A youngster who feels close to his father will probably want to be just like dear old Dad—no matter what dear old

Dad is really like. For example, to my customary query "What does your father do for a living?" one bright second grader said:

"Nothing!"

"Doesn't he work?" I asked in surprise.

"Nope!"

"Doesn't he like *any* kind of work?" I was trying to give Dad a break.

"Sure," said junior. "He likes *easy* work once in a long while."

Well, that father may not be setting any worlds on fire, but at least he had a loving and loyal son, which is more important than making money, when you stop to think of it.

The seven-year-old child of a famous movie star unconsciously revealed the conditioning his surroundings had worked on his philosophy of life. He had told me that he wanted to be an actor in motion pictures and when I asked him why, a blissful expression spread across his face. "I'd like the life," he confided.

"What would that be like?" I asked him cautiously.

"Well," he said, "a movie star wakes up at ten and has breakfast in bed. Then he takes a limousine to the studio and kisses girls all day. Then he has dinner in some nightclub, and if he wants to, he marries the prettiest girl late that night."

I didn't try to disillusion him. But I had a lot of fun with his father the next day on the phone.

Truth is not only stranger than fiction but a whole lot funnier. Kids don't waste any words when they set out to tell the truth about their families. Here are some shortshorts.

"What can your dad do around the house?"
"Well, once he tried to fix the car."
"What happened?"
"We had to get a new car."

* * * *

"What do you want to be when you grow up?"
"An airline hostess."
"Why?"
"Because my aunt was one and she told me you can marry rich millionaires."
"Who'd your aunt marry?"
"The airport janitor."

* * * *

"What do you want to be?"
"A fireman."
"Why pick that?"
"Because my dad says I'm dumb enough to be one."
"What does your dad do?"
"He's a fireman."

* * * *

"What makes your mother the maddest?"
"When my dad comes home, takes off his shoes, opens a bottle of beer, sits down in front of the TV set, and whistles at all the pretty girls on the program."

* * * *

"What's the funniest thing you've seen this summer?"

"Dad came home, hit Mom on the back of her lap with a chair, and she threw a cherry pie at him."

*   *   *   *

"What does your dad do for fun?"

"He chases cats."

"What does your mother do for fun?"

"She puts ice cubes in my father's beer while he's out chasing cats."

*   *   *   *

"Do you have any brothers or sisters?"

"No."

"Did you ask for one?"

"Yes."

"What did your mother say?"

"Maybe in a month or so when Dad gets rested up."

* * * *

"Who's the boss in your house?"

"My mother. Because she's the one who tells Daddy where he can go!"

* * * *

"I hear your father's an actor," I began with one typical Hollywood boy. "What kind of an actor?"

"A TV actor."

"And what kind of parts does he play?"

"I don't know," he said sadly. "They're so bad that Mom won't let us look."

The artless honesty of children can be devastating in the so-called "polite society" of grownups, where telling a simple truth can be like pulling the pin on a hand grenade. Girls seem to understand this need to guard their tongue quite early in life, but boys push onward, blurting out exactly what they think. One of my truth-telling heroes is a little boy who was attending his regular Saturday afternoon dancing class. He was obviously feeling ill at ease that day, so the dancing master walked over, pointed to a girl nearby, and suggested that the boy ask her to dance. The boy nodded his head, approached the girl, and off they danced. A few moments later the dancing master saw the girl haul off and give the boy a resounding whack in the face. The boy abandoned her in the middle of the dance floor and walked off looking bewildered. The dancing master asked him,

"What on earth happened?" "I don't know," said the boy. "I just told her while we were dancing that for a fat girl she sure didn't sweat much."

Not so long ago tax assessors in many parts of the country would ring every doorbell and inspect every stick of furniture in the house so that they could figure out how much to tax you on your personal property. If you knew the assessor was in the neighborhood making his rounds, it became a game—hiding as many of your assets as possible. One day the parents of a friend of mine had seen the assessor coming, so they struggled like stevedores to hide an enormous expensive radio in the closet. Moments later the official arrived with his pencil and paper and began noting the contents of the house. As he was leaving, the smallest member of the family, a five-year-old boy, looked up at his father and said, "Hey, Dad! You forgot to tell him about the radio in the closet."

Glancing out of her upstairs window, a woman noticed that her next-door neighbor was about to ring her doorbell. Having a busy day ahead and not wanting to spend the whole morning chatting, the woman told her little boy to go tell the neighbor that she was out, so when the doorbell rang, the boy answered, "Hello, Mrs. Brown, my mommy is out." "Oh, that's too bad," said Mrs. Brown. "I just came to borrow some sugar." The boy turned and yelled up the stairs, "Hey, Mom! When you said to tell Mrs. Brown you were out, did you mean you were out of sugar?"

Teaching children to be polite is a precarious business. They learn the delicate art of saying the right thing soon enough, but it's not automatic as it is with adults. The truth never lies too far beneath the surface, as in this story:

A mother took her family to her sister's house for dinner. As they were leaving, her six-year-old said, "Thank you for the pie." The sister beamed at the compliment but pushed her luck by saying, "Did you really like it or are you just being polite?" The child beamed back, proud that his good manners had been appreciated, and said, "Just being polite."

Honesty isn't the only dangerous virtue in a small child. Another is family loyalty. A Hollywood woman's family was about ready to check out of a plush hotel when their four-year-old boy got into the shower and was soaked. So mother grabbed two big hotel towels to wrap his wet things in. She had planned to return the towels, but living miles away, she never did—and just used them around the house. A year later the family returned to the hotel. Just as the husband was giving the hotel boy a tip, the little boy said, "Don't give that man money. The people in this hotel are thieves! They have our best bath towels strung all over the bathroom!"

To the dangerous virtues of honesty and loyalty in children we must also add helpful concern for one's elders. Put yourself in the place of a woman who had a headache one afternoon and her nine-year-old daughter wanted to do something to make her feel better. Finally Mother told the girl she could make her a cup of tea. After quite a while the girl brought it, and Mother drank it gratefully. "You've been very helpful, dear," said Mother. "You did a good job of straining the tea, too." The girl smiled prouldy. "I couldn't find the strainer, Mom, so I had to use the fly swatter." Noticing the horrified look spreading over her mother's face, the little girl reassured her: "Oh, don't worry. I didn't use the brand-new swatter. I used the *old* one!"

There's something especially pleasing when the red spotlight of an embarrassing moment plays across a schoolteacher, a preacher, or a judge. Somewhere, deep down inside each of us, there lurks a resentment toward the kind of person whose job it is to tell us we should be better, do better, and know more. It's the same rebellion against authority that prompts the American baseball crowd to yell, "Kill the ump!"

Therefore, whenever I have a child on the program whose father fits one of those "holier than thou" categories, I bear down a little bit harder on my cross-examination. Imagine the delight of millions of former students when a boy told me why he thought he had been picked out of his entire class to be on the show.

"My teacher likes my daddy."

"How do you know?"

"Because when my daddy comes to school to pick me up every afternoon, my teacher walks me out to the car and he pinches her in some of the funniest places."

When I asked another child why she was picked she said:

"Because my father is the superintendent of schools and knows everything."

"If he knows so much," I continued, "what advice did he give you this morning?"

"He told me when I'm up here on stage not to scratch, no matter where it itches."

Sometimes the dialogue gets so fascinating that I hate to break it off—especially when the child is a P.K. (preacher's kid) as I was:

"What do you want to be when you grow up?"

"A preacher like my father."

"What does he do most of the time?"

"He talks Christians into becoming Methodists."

"Do you think he could get me into heaven?" I raised a hurdle. "After all, you know, I'm a Baptist."

"That would be hard for lots of them, but not *my* daddy. He'd just put you on a Methodist jet plane and shoot you up there."

"Where is heaven?" I asked wonderingly.

"Oh, it's about twenty miles past Mars."

"What do you think it looks like?" I persisted.

"Everyone's lying around on big pink clouds eating angel food."

"Baptists, too?" I cautioned.

"They get smaller pieces."

And somewhere out in the listening audience dozens of ministers had the text for their sermon on the following Sunday.

Another time a delightful five-year-old told me she'd like to be a nun when she grew up. I asked her what a nun was, and she rattled off this interesting and offbeat description: "A nun is a lady who goes down the street in pairs."

The all-time high for fun with Catholic sisters happened when two charming nuns brought some four-year-olds for a visit. We began the "on the air" conversation as one of the tiny girls pointed out in the audience and said she liked school most when the sister told Bible stories. While the sister self-consciously lowered her head in becoming modesty, I complimented her and said that I'd be interested in which Bible story was the little girl's favorite. Thus began a lively conversation which none of us who heard it will ever forget.

"Tell me your favorite story that the sister tells you," I encouraged.

"The story of Edem and Ave." It almost sounded right the way she pronounced their names so confidently. As the audience tittered in appreciation, I went on as if nothing were wrong:

"And who were Edem and Ave?"

"They were two bare people who liked each other." The audience laughter was beginning to build, and the sweet child's face began to look at me questioningly.

"So far you are doing just fine," I encouraged her. "What did these two bare people do?"

"They lived in a public park."

"Did they work for a living?" I hastily went on to hold the mood.

"Oh, yes. They swept the sidewalk and kept the swimming pool clean."

"And then what happened?" I held her glance firmly on mine and kept a straight face throughout.

"The girl kept eating the cherries off the bush when she shouldn't."

I stole a glance into the audience to check if the sister was still there. She *was* and, mouth slightly open, was totally entranced by this interpretation of what went on in the Garden of Eden.

"What happened next?"

"God was mad at them and He was going to punish them. But they hided under a bush. But they couldn't fool God and He found them." Her voice was rising as she was caught up in her story.

"Go on," I urged.

"So God decided to punish them twice."

"Twice?" I echoed.

"Yes, Mr. Winkwetter. First He sent them both straight down to hell." She paused at the enormity of the thought, and then delivered the coup de grâce:

"And then he changed them into Protestants!"

The whoops and yells from the audience rolled across the stage in waves that were almost physical. The sister was convulsed along with everyone else. The four-year-old darling sat up and looked around with the expression of one who had just passed a difficult test with a mark of 100. Which she had!

Kids of nursery-school age take things very literally. When a three-year-old girl was told she must be very quiet in church because it was "God's house," the girl asked, "Where does he sleep? On the benches?"

Another little girl came home from parochial school one

day and told the family that "the sea monster" had visited her class. The family finally figured out who the visitor was—the Monsigneur.

Parents sometimes forget that they are a constant living example for their children. As the proverb says, "Little pitchers have big ears." And after listening to what we do, they go into action themselves, like the little boy who sat down to dinner with the family and some visiting relatives. Several of the guests were already digging in when the three-year-old boy suddenly pounded on the table and said, "Damn it, we forgot to say the prayer!"

In preparing for company, a woman told her four-year-old daughter not to touch anything on the coffee table—or else. When the first guests came, the mother served them each a cocktail—but forgot to pass the coasters around. One glass left a telltale ring, and the little girl told the drinker, "You'd better clean that up before my mother takes your pants down and spanks your bottom."

Even the children themselves are occasionally flabbergasted at what they've just said. One five-year-old on my show was explaining how to have good manners at lunch, and he concluded with the sweeping statement:

"And if you've got to throw up, throw up on yourself."

The gale of laughter reddened his face and he slunk down into his chair like any grownup caught in a boo-boo.

An older child, a girl of almost ten, was so vehement in her dislike for boys that she was betrayed into a red-faced moment after this exchange:

"What do you want to be when you grow up?"

"I'd like to be a mother and have three children."

"What kind of a boy would you like to have for a husband?"

"Oh, I wouldn't want to be married." And with this she suddenly covered her face while we all had a hilarious thirty seconds at her expense.

Nothing delights an audience more than to see the rug pulled out from under me for a change. I won't forget this little lady in a hurry:

"What do you want to be?"

"Just a plain old housewife."

"What kind of husband do you want?"

"Just a plain old man."

"Well, give us an example of a plain old man."

"*You!*"

I don't imagine it's very easy to embarrass a Navy admiral, but a niece of mine managed it when an admiral called on her family in Mission Beach, California. They were all going out to a party, so he arrived in full-dress uniform, looking very imposing with all his ribbons, medals, and gold braid. The little girl answered the doorbell, and when she saw this tremendous apparition, this fantastic character standing at the doorway, she turned around and gasped out to her mother, "I don't know who is at the door—but I think it's God!"

I'm grateful to a Florida woman for this story about her four-year-old grandson, Geoffrey: He got up one morning dragging his leg, but his mother couldn't find anything wrong with him. This went on for two days, but he didn't complain of any pain. On the third day his worried mother took him to her pediatrician. The doctor checked him carefully but couldn't find anything amiss. He checked him again the next day and sent him to the children's hospital where he was X-rayed and examined by pediatric specialists who could find nothing wrong. Geoffrey still walked dragging one leg. After two more days of this and eighty-five dollars' worth of doctor and laboratory bills, one doctor asked him, "Geoffrey, why do you have to drag one leg when you walk?" The boy replied, "I'm Chester. I work for Mr. Dillon."

3

Blushers at Work

If there is one place where we all push hardest to make a good impression, it's on the job. Everyone rides on the merry-go-round of job prestige, from the banker who adorns his office with his name and title in gold leaf to the truck driver who stencils his name on the cab door. Whether our collars are white or blue, we all try to appear at our best while working. The few exceptions to this last are such "in" outsiders as the guitar twangers and banjo pickers of our coffeehouses, who must be careful about looking suitably unkempt. So with everything at stake, our daily livelihood and our ambitions as well, we all try to fit in and stand out at the same time. At this point an upside-down kind of law takes over, and that's where the fun begins. The higher we climb, the faster we slide. So let's see what happens to the climbers and sliders on company time.

I remember the backstage consternation the day Arthur Godfrey and I emceed the first Pillsbury National Bake-Off, a live telecast of a $100,000 competition involving scores of housewives and teen-age girls assembled in the Grand Ballroom of the Waldorf Astoria. Each contestant was a state finalist and had just baked or cooked some specialty which was then taken to the judges. Arthur and I were to give the prizes.

When a Junior National Award winner came up, Arthur and I congratulated the girl and said, "Here is your check." But as we displayed her prize creation to the audience, the girl spoke up, loud and clear: "That ain't mine!" There was a long pause while Arthur and I stared at each other. Then I laughed and said, "That's very funny—but this is what you baked." She stood her ground. "I never saw that before and it's not mine! I guess I ought to know what I made." We proceeded to have an argument, right on the air before millions of viewers. She absolutely refused to take the check, and we were completely baffled. In desperation we looked over at the judges, and they kept signaling that it *was* hers. Finally a home economist stepped forward and solved the mystery, confessing, "We baked it a different shape and gave it another name. It is a banana cream whatsis you baked, isn't it, miss?" "Yes," said the girl. So at last she took the money and walked away mad.

An embarrassing verbal slip that brought me a lot of mail occurred early in my career when I was broadcasting from the World's Fair in 1939 in San Francisco. The show was called the "Roma Wine World's Fair Party," and I was interviewing a young couple about to be married. They agreed to have the actual ceremony performed on our stage the following week.

So at the conclusion of the broadcast I adlibbed this gay farewell: "Be sure to be listening or be here in person next week, when this happy young couple will consummate their wedding vows right here on this stage." I *thought* that I was saying in a more interesting way that they would plight their troth on stage. We had one of the largest crowds in the history of the Fair the following week, watching with consummate interest.

Another embarrassing broadcast for me was when I was doing "man on the street" shows at the Dallas Centennial Exposition. It was early evening, and nobody was around, so I had to fill in time. I was becoming a bit desperate when a man walked out of a nearby restaurant. I thought this was my salvation, so I grabbed him by the shoulder and said, "Having any fun at the Fair?" And he retorted, "What the hell do you want?" He was a belligerent drunk, and the more I tried to get away from him, the more belligerent he became. Finally I gave the mike to the engineer after saying, "Excuse me, folks. This will take just a moment." And that's how long it took to send my profane antagonist to dreamland. Embarrassing? Or course. Necessary? Who knows?

Emcees and announcers run a daily risk of saying the wrong thing, like the broadcaster who assured his listeners, "I always delve into these products before I tell you about them, and today I'm going to talk about bloomers." One of my worst moments didn't involve *what* I said, but how I said it. A prankster pal of mine came into the radio studio in San Diego when I was doing a commercial, and tried to break me up with a pantomime about a drunk and a fire hydrant. He did. I giggled. I snorted. And finally I gave up and roared with laughter through the rest of the commercial announcement. No sponsor considers his message *that* funny. But the one I had picked was a lulu. It was Benbough's Mortuary. And the sales pitch was for the newest, finest, most reasonable cremation services.

I couldn't possibly remember all the embarrassing things that have happened to me on stage over the years, but this

I do know—a great many of them involved animals that we used in various stunts on "People Are Funny." We used just about every animal you can think of, from eagles to elephants, and they all waited until they came on stage to behave just as you might expect—and fear—they would. The most memorable one by all odds was a stunt with the world's strongest man, who could lift an elephant on his back. We built a gigantic platform, all trussed and braced so that he could get underneath it and then lift the entire platform, elephant and all, up in the air. The elephant ponderously heaved himself up on the platform some four feet off the stage. The world's strongest man bent his back for the record-breaking lift. The orchestra trumpeted a fanfare. And then came the historical reprise to Louis XV—"*Après moi, le déluge!*" Even Noah and his Ark would not have stood the test—and neither did we!

Rather than face up to embarrassment, either to oneself or to others, the average human being will do all kinds of strange things and submit to almost any indignity. In fact I did a whole show called "The Art Linkletter Show" on NBC a couple of years ago, based on the fact that people feel so reluctant about putting somebody else in an embarrassing situation that they will get into an even worse situation themselves. We would hire actors and actresses to get people into situations, and see how far we could push them. ("Candid Camera" has done this quite often.)

Once we sent an actor to a very nice Hollywood restaurant. He walked over to a booth where a diner was sitting with his girl friend, and said, "I beg your pardon. I hate to intrude, but I noticed you are eating something on the menu that I love to eat, but cannot if it happens to have even the faintest trace of certain kinds of seasonings in it. Would

you mind if I sampled a small bit of yours?" The man
and the girl were both startled by this, yet they didn't want
to cause any problems, so they agreed. Our man took a bite
and said, "Oh, it's very good! And while I'm here, do you
mind if I have just a taste of . . ." and he took a sample
of everything they had ordered. These two people were more
and more uncomfortable while he was eating food off both
their plates, yet they never stopped him! What would you
have done? Punched him in the nose? Want to bet? People
in public hate any kind of embarrassment.

Another time involved a man checking for his mail at
the desk of a large downtown Los Angeles hotel, when a
maharajah dressed in a complete East Indian outfit appeared
at his elbow. The maharajah, of course, was our actor, and
so was the desk clerk. "I've enjoyed my stay here very much,"
the maharajah told the clerk. "Would you mind giving this
to the housekeeper to express my appreciation?" He put a
string of jewels down on the counter—cut and uncut diamonds and rubies! "Keep some for yourself," he added. The
guest watching all this was absolutely flabbergasted. The maharajah noticed him staring and said, "Do you like this
ruby?," holding up a huge stone. "It's beautiful," said the
guest. "Have it," said the maharajah. "Oh, no," said the man.
"Take it," said the maharajah. "In my country this is the
essence of hospitality. When somebody sees something they
like, you give it to them." The guest looked up at the desk
clerk, wondering what to do. The clerk nodded and murmured, "Go ahead and take it—very important for our diplomatic relations." So the man took it and thanked the
potentate profusely. Then the maharajah started away and
suddenly turned back, saying, "What a beautiful tie you have
on." He stood there expectantly, and this very well-dressed

middle-aged man took the tie off and gave it to him. Then the maharajah said, "That shirt. It's a wonderful shirt." The man looked around sheepishly and finally said, "Well, I really shouldn't take it off here in the lobby—but if you'll wait a minute, I'll run upstairs and bring it back to you."

Sometimes a program stunt would backfire, and the joke would be on us. I'll never forget the time we sent a woman contestant out of our "People Are Funny" studios to a big

Hollywood hotel. She was to drop notes out of the window on which were scribbled in lipstick, "Am being held by kidnapers in Room 617. . . . Help!" Sure enough, a sailor went by, found one of the notes, came roaring upstairs, pounded on the door, and "rescued" her. We brought him back to the studio and rewarded him for his courage. Unknown to us, however, several of the frantic notes our contestant had written had fallen on the ledges of the hotel building. They stayed there on the ledges for several nights, until a breeze from a different direction blew them off into the street below. By then Room 617 was occupied by a paying guest, completely oblivious to the trick that fate had prepared for her. "Open the door or we'll break it down!" came the gruff orders of a policeman outside the door. And while the poor lady shook in her nightgown, the would-be rescuers ransacked the place for the "kidnapers." When the uproar was over, we had a lot of explaining to do to the lady and the police.

Doing a show without a script has its own special hazards, as my son Jack learned when he was emceeing the Miss Universe contest back in 1965. Jack had questions carefully worked out for each of the semifinalists because none of them spoke English. They had been coached to understand and answer certain specific questions. Just as the show went on the air and the announcer said, "Here is your master of ceremonies," a stagehand bumped into Jack, knocking all his written questions to the floor. Jack walked on stage, bowed, and did his interviews entirely adlib. It was a frantic night. "What is your name?" Jack asked one South American girl. "I am nineteen of the years old," she replied. "Do you like United States men?" he asked. "Two brothers and three sisters," she said. The right answers never did catch up with the right questions.

If you're clever and resourceful, you can often swivel-hip your way out of an otherwise awkward on-the-job situation. A young dentist who had just set up his practice in a small town was equal to the challenge when he got a call from a patient who had just left him an hour before. He could barely understand her as she mumbled, "How wong do oo want me to weave iss wad of cotton in my mouf?" He flushed, realizing he had forgotten to remove the cotton after finishing her filling, but his professional presence of mind didn't desert him. "Leave it in another thirty minutes," he advised, "and then remove it." "Fank oo, dokker," said the grateful patient, and hung up.

Ministers are also presumed to be perfect, but they will all confess to falling somewhat short of that graceful state.

One man of the cloth in Birmingham, Alabama, a Southern
Baptist like myself, was baptizing a young girl in a river when
he lost his grip and dropped her. As he frantically fished
around for her, the youngster swam right between his legs
and made for shore. The minister made a dive for her,
caught her, and went on with the ceremony.

Another minister up in Oregon was assigned to a new
church and was making the rounds of his new parishioners.
At one home he asked a little boy where his mother was,
and the youngster pointed to a door. He knocked and the
lady inside, thinking it was the child, said, "Come in and
be quiet." The minister did come in and he was very quiet.
In fact, he couldn't think of anything to say as he backed
out the door, because the lady was in the tub.

During World War II, workers desiring defense plant jobs
had to bring their birth certificates along when they went in
for interviews at employment service offices. A woman who
was an interviewer in those days recalls what happened as
she returned to work after her honeymoon. Looking up at
an applicant, she asked him, "Did you bring along your
birth control certificate?" He looked thunderstruck, and she
backed hastily out of the interviewing booth and found another worker to finish the interview. Later her boss heard
the story and commented, "Don't tell me we have to carry
cards around now for that, too."

There's a story they tell on the West Coast about a wartime defense worker who came straight off a farm to a job
as a welder at a huge shipyard. His first assignment was
to use his torch to cut a circular hole in the deck for a
hatch. He marked the circle and was doing a beautiful job,
but when he finished he let out a yell and disappeared from
sight. It seems he had been kneeling inside the circle as he

worked—and when he finished, he and the metal both
dropped to the next deck.

Do you get flustered when someone stands over you while
you are working? A new switchboard operator was understandably jittery when her boss's wife came and stood behind
her, watching every move. The girl managed to survive until
the lady walked off. Sighing in relief, the girl reached for
her earpiece to take an incoming call. At least she thought
it was her earpiece, but it was an inkwell. The bright blue
ink went gurgling into her ear, down her neck, and onto
her dress. Red-faced and blue-eared, she stayed at her post
until lunchtime, when she went out for a good bath and a
change of clothes.

A waitress in Hyde Park, Massachusetts, couldn't take her
eyes off a handsome fellow who sat down at one of her
tables and ordered coffee. She returned and said, "Here you
are, sir," still gazing soulfully into his eyes. Meanwhile the
cup slowly slid off the saucer—and the coffee cascaded right
into his lap! He leaped up as the steamy liquid soaked his
pants, and began dancing about while she apologized. By
the time he had cooled off from the coffee, he warmed up
to her and asked her for a date. Now she pours his coffee
everyday, because they got married.

On her first day of teaching grammar school, a young
woman in Torrance, California, was introducing herself to
some first graders, telling the children how she hoped they'd
all get to know each other better. Just then she backed up
against the blackboard map, which rolled up like a window
shade and pulled her skirt clear up past her waist. The class
was very quiet as she struggled until she detached herself
from the map and got her skirt back down again. Then one

little boy broke the silence by saying, "We know you better already."

An inspector with the Los Angeles County Fire Department was asked to talk to a group of grammar schoolers. He was introduced as an inspector of the Fire Department, showed a film about the department, answered questions about fires, and just as the inspector was leaving, a little boy in the front row said, "Say—are you a cop?"

A teen-age girl was working in a St. Louis department

store when a parcel chute was installed. The other girls dared her to be the first "parcel." She took the dare and went sliding down to the bottom—where she knocked over her waiting boss.

A San Francisco woman remembers riding a cable car en route to a job interview. A large man got aboard, lost his balance, stepped on her brand-new shoes, and hurt her foot. She said, "Oh, you big ox!" Later as she waited for her interview, the receptionist said, "You may go in now." Behind the desk was the "big ox." End of interview.

Another young lady applied for a job requiring a good memory, so she assured the personnel director that hers was excellent. She came away certain she'd get the job, but she didn't—not after returning to his office for the umbrella she left behind.

It was a lazy summer day, much too beautiful to be wasted on work, so a young executive telephoned his office that he was "ill" and just couldn't come in. Then he tossed his golf bag into the car, went off to the club—and found he was teamed up with his boss and the company brass.

One of the most colorful newspapermen in Los Angeles was a fellow we'll call Frank. He was one of the finest writers on the paper, but he was hopelessly addicted to betting on the horses. He was the lost, abandoned type of bettor who would stuff up the holes in his shoes with yesterday's racing form and then try to borrow two dollars from his landlady for the next race. One afternoon Frank had a long shot riding, and by nightfall everyone in the office had heard about his fantastic good luck. Frank's horse had romped in by two lengths, paying 80 to 1! Frank sat at his typewriter in a daze all afternoon, dreaming of all those dollars that would pay the rent and the grocery bill. Then the phone rang. It was one of the beat reporters. "I've got a little paragraph for you, Frank," he said. "The vice squad just knocked over another bookie. He has an odd name, so I'll spell it—S-A-V . . ." Frank's smile faded. "Never mind spelling it," Frank said sadly. "I know how."

Another reporter was sent out at Christmastime in a Salvation Army uniform, to ring the bell over the little chimney and do a story about the good people who came by to drop in their donations for the poor. He had a good day and then turned in his collection to the Salvation Army supervisor. On the way back to his office, however, the reporter realized he had no money of his own—just a raging thirst for a double martini. So he walked into the nearest bar, took off his Salvation Army cap, and went down the line of bar stools to ask for donations. The folks at the bar, like drinkers everywhere who feel a twinge of conscience when they see a clerical collar, gave generously of their quarters and dollars. "Bless you, brethren," said the reporter as the money rained into his cap. Then he reached the end of the bar, turned the cap over, piled up the money, and said, "Give me a double martini on the rocks." He was nearly mobbed by the outraged patrons before the barkeep stepped in and identified him as a columnist with a pixie sense of humor.

A woman working as a substitute switchboard operator in an oil refinery plant was told exactly how to summon various executives to the phone by blowing the steam whistle, in code. In came a call for the superintendent, so she blew the whistle for him. Within seconds the superintendent burst into her office with the entire fire department on his heels. The signal button she'd pressed had stuck—and a continuous whistle meant a fire.

A young lady at a huge aircraft manufacturing plant got one of those forbidden personal calls—and this one was really personal. She was having some spicy fun, whispering confidences and giggling, until she looked around and saw the entire building was in an uproar. Her supposedly private call had gotten plugged into the vast plant's intercom system, and her cozy little intimacies were being broadcast to thousands of her fellow workers.

A woman working in the men's department of a downtown store sold a gentleman a pair of pants. They had to be shortened, so he was told to come back in two days. When he came back he walked up to her and said, "Are you the one I got the pants off of Saturday afternoon?" She said yes—and then turned to see the utterly stricken face of a floorwalker who overheard them.

A registered nurse stopped a man at the door of the maternity delivery room. "You're not going in there, sir!" she told him. "But I have to get in there," he protested. "Oh, no, you don't," she said. "Absolutely nobody goes in there but the doctor." The man sighed. "I am the doctor."

Another nurse showed a newborn infant to the man she thought was the father. "The baby looks just like you," she said. The man looked very uncomfortable. Then she learned that the baby's father was a farmer, and the fellow she congratulated was his hired man. Wow!

Two Indian patients were brought in for a student nurse to put to bed. One protested, but this wasn't unusual, so she insisted that they both get into bed. Two days later, when the Indian Affairs doctor made his rounds, he discovered the Indian who objected had brought the other one in for treatment. (Evidently all the Indians had blanket coverage.)

A woman census taker still blushes to think of the day

she spent fifteen minutes arguing through the door with some stubborn character who kept yelling back and wouldn't let her in. Finally she realized the voice behind the door belonged to . . . a parrot.

I remember the day I was fired from the most important job I had ever had, as the radio director of the San Francisco World's Fair on Treasure Island in 1939. I was planning the opening of the Fair for broadcast on at least two of the major radio networks and had devised a number of what I thought were rather interesting and dramatic events. This program had been sent for approval to the general manager of the Fair, an elderly, forceful, and very authoritative man. He called me into the office shortly afterward and dressed me down. "Linkletter," he said, "these plans are completely without imagination. This is a very plebeian, plodding, unimaginative script." What could I say, except what I did: "Perhaps you have a better suggestion." He looked at me scornfully. "Of course I do," he said. "I wouldn't dream of tearing something down without rebuilding in its place." Then he launched into his own pet scheme. "To match the magnificence and beauty of this Fair," he said, "we must have an opening that could be done by using the Golden Gate Bridge as a giant Aeolian harp, playing our theme song, 'California, Here I Come,' as we go on the air." I said, "That is quite a project. What do you propose to do?" He said, "We will string microphones across the bridge—hundreds of microphones. Each one of them will pick up the sound made by the wind as it comes across the Pacific Ocean and passes across the cables that hold up the bridge. Each cable has a different tension, and each tension will produce a different note. Our engineers will man gigantic consoles with hundreds of dials, and as they twist these dials, bringing these tones in and out in various combinations, they will play the song—using the bridge as a harp." I said, "Mr. Director, you're nuts!" He said, "Mr. Linkletter, you're fired!" And that was the start of my career as a free-lance, independent producer.

4

Pants à Go-go

The greatest sight gag of all time is seeing someone's pants fall down. No matter how often you see it happen, it will always be funny. You will laugh even if you know it's going to happen, you're told it's going to happen, and you see the person it's going to happen to, and you know that he knows it's going to happen! That's how basic and fundamental the idea is. I'd say that fully sixty per cent of the thousands of letters that reached me during the preparation for this book had to do with the precipitate descent of somebody's drawers in public—on a main street, a crowded elevator, in a department store, while running to catch a bus, and even in church.

Pants-dropping is such a surefire laugh getter that we used it for years in the warm-up of my "People Are Funny" show, to make sure we started with plenty of hilarity. Moments before the show got under way I would tell the audience, "Mr. Guedel, the father of our producer, will come out to lead the applause. When he jumps up in the air, his pants will fall off, and you will laugh. In fact, you won't be able to stop laughing, and that will be the way we'll go on the air." So the red light would go on, this rather distinguished gray-haired gentleman would run up to the middle of the stage, jump up in the air, his pants would fall off—and the audience would roll in the aisles.

One of the longest sustained laughs in the history of broadcasting happened on the show of the one and only Groucho Marx. He asked a guest to tell his most embarrassing moment. "I was rooming at a hotel with a big fat friend," the man told Groucho. "My fat friend was out late, and he had left his trousers and shoes on his bed. I was asleep when I heard the fire engines coming. I didn't have anything on, so I looked around, half asleep, and put on my pal's pants and shoes. Meanwhile the firemen were putting a big ladder up to my window. I got on the ladder and there was a huge crowd down below. I went about three rungs down, and my shoe slipped. I reached for it—and lost my pants. It was very embarrassing, Groucho," the man added, "because everybody down there in the crowd could see my predicament."

Another gentleman in New Jersey was trying to impress his date with an elaborate dinner in a very fine restaurant that featured a plush mid-Victorian décor. They'd had such a wonderful meal that the young man loosened not only his belt, but his top button on the pants to his tuxedo. After dessert and coffee, with the violins playing in a hushed and genteel atmosphere, the couple got up to leave. The scraping of their chairs turned every diner's head toward them, just as the young man's pants plummeted to the floor around his ankles!

There he stood like a man of distinction in an underwear ad as the entire restaurant rocked with hilarity. Even the music stopped, because the musicians found that playing

violin while choking with laughter is about as easy as whis-
tling with a mouth full of crackers.

As long as we're drawer-dropping, we certainly should tell
the story sent me by a lady who says, "My husband bought
me a lovely pair of red nylon panties. That evening we
were visiting my brother, his wife, and their grown son,
and they were showing us some new things they had gotten
that day. I jumped up and said, 'Let me show you all something real pretty I have—and I yanked my dress up to show
them the panties, and remembered an instant too late I had
forgotten to put them on. Boy, that brought the house down—
and me, too!"

Ranking close behind the loss of one's pants must surely be
the malfunctioning of that marvelous but sometimes treacherous invention known as the zipper. The particular zipper
causing the most social anxiety, of course, is the one known
to trouser manufacturers as the slide fastener of the fly.
Take my word for it, there is absolutely no way for a man
to maintain his dignity once he discovers that his fly is stuck
at half-mast. I'm sure one of the first performers who would
agree with me on this shattering fact is my fellow emcee,
one of the most versatile men in show business today, Garry
Moore. Perhaps you were watching, as I was, that day years
ago when Garry had a daytime TV show and was doing a
feature on Bermuda shorts for men.

It was a live show, and in the haste of changing costumes
in the wings Garry emerged with his entire fly down—right
to the very last notch. He was glibly doing one of his famous
monologues, and getting much more than his usual share of
laughs, when he happened to turn and see some frantic
arm-waving offstage. He looked down at himself, looked up,
then turned about with an instantaneous zip—and became

once more the debonair Garry, carrying off with great aplomb
an incident that might have left a lesser man fumbling for
an exit as well as his zipper.

If I had to pick one embarrassing story about zippers, my
favorite would be about the plump gentleman who had a
big dinner, went to the movies, and slid his zipper down to
be more comfortable. A lady as plump as he came pushing
her way past him. She couldn't get by, so he stood up to
allow her to pass. As he did so, he naturally pulled up his
zipper. Just then she moved and caught the back of her
dress in his fly. In the semidarkness neither realized at first
what had happened. She tried to keep moving, and felt herself being held back. He also felt a tug and couldn't figure
out why she wouldn't move out of his way. They were both
stuck. At last what had happened became obvious, and two
very embarrassed individuals began wiggling back and forth.
He tried to get his zipper down, but it wouldn't move because its metal teeth had a deathlike grip on her dress. Now
everybody in the whole aisle had to get up and go into the
main aisle to make room for them to escape. The gentleman
and his indignant prisoner backed out and then up the main
aisle to the manager's office in a reverse lockstep. There they
were, two complete strangers, fastened together by a zipper.
It's hard to imagine a longer lasting, more embarrassing situation than that!

Fathers of brides are notoriously more nervous than the
brides themselves. I know, because I played that role myself
for my daughter Dawn, about two grandchildren ago. So
I can sympathize with a gentleman who overslept on the
morning of his daughter's wedding and dashed wildly about,
putting on his formal attire for the big ceremony. He reached
for the glass where his teeth had spent the night, dashed into

the bathroom, and then watched in disbelief as his dentures slipped and shattered on the tile floor. What to do? He tried telephoning the dentist for a spare set, but the molar master was off on vacation. Panicky, Dad could just picture himself being stared at by scores of wedding guests as he escorted his daughter down the aisle. They would be sure to see he had no teeth, wouldn't they? Feeling trapped, he looked into the bathroom mirror and practiced puffing out his cheeks so they wouldn't look so hollow. It seemed to help, so he finished dressing and joined the family procession to church.

When Dad's big moment came, and the organ played the bride's processional, Dad adjusted his smile and paraded his daughter to the altar. He was even smiling until the minister intoned the traditional question "Who giveth this woman?" Dad gulped. He had forgotten he had a speaking role in the ritual. Finally he managed a mushy "I do."

Then came the reception. Dentureless Dad stood mutely in line, shaking hands and nodding with his odd little smile. Later on he overheard a guest say, "Your father is a handsome-looking man but he certainly doesn't say much. I didn't hear a word out of him all afternoon."

Husbands and wives aren't supposed to have secrets from each other, I'm told, but a new bride in Washington hadn't told her groom that she wore dentures. One day he asked her if she'd come into town with him. To her surprise, they stopped off at his dentist's for an appointment he had made. She waited in the anteroom while he was being checked over. Then he emerged and said, "As long as we're here, darling, the dentist might as well look at your teeth, too." She protested but her husband insisted until she finally went in. Once safe in the privacy of the dentist's office, she confessed her awful secret. The dentist looked at her in quiet amusement for a moment and then said, "The real reason for your visit today is an excuse for me to break the news to you that your *husband* doesn't have a tooth left. *He* wears dentures." So she decided to "gum" clean with her husband.

Here are a few more denture misadventures and whoppers about choppers:

A family in Chicago Heights, Illinois, had gone out on Mother's Day for a special dinner. The waitress came to their table to get their order, but as she bent over the table, her upper plate fell out, caromed off the host's head—and landed in his dish. The waitress disappeared with both his plate and hers, and another girl came out for their order.

I admire the quick thinking and dexterity of a Canadian woman who was playing the part of a French maid in an amateur theatrical. As she walked on stage for her lines, her front partial went flying out. She reached out and made a Willie Mays catch, put the partial back in place, and went on without missing a line! Evidently her feat became known around town, because the next night several playgoers said they were disappointed that this particular bit of juggling wasn't in the show.

While traveling on an overnight train a lady put her upper plate under her pillow. The next morning she couldn't find it, so she struggled into her clothes in the narrow berth and finally went off to breakfast. Later, as she took her seat in the dining car, she felt a sharp bite on her posterior. She'd "bitten" herself with the missing molars.

As all denture wearers know, it takes several trips to the dentist before the new teeth feel comfortable. An Ohio lady understood this and didn't mind all the trouble it took to see her dentist, even though on this particular day it was bitterly cold, and it took three hours on as many buses to

reach his office. At last she was sitting down in his chair. "Open your mouth, please," said the dentist. She did—and she had forgotten to bring along her teeth.

An internationally known Hollywood film columnist once told me of the time she was a guest at a state dinner in Argentina, in the days before Dictator Juan Perón was

booted out. Perón was presiding at the table, surrounded
by dignitaries, diplomats, and bemedaled generals. During
the main course the columnist was horrified to discover that
the cap on her front tooth had disappeared. Holding her
hand over her mouth to hide the pointed spike where the
cap had fit, she fumbled about on the table and searched
through her food. No luck. At last she saw it gleaming at
her from across the table, on the plate of a general. At
any second, it was obvious, he would be chewing on her
tooth. Frantically she explained the situation to an English-
speaking Argentine, who halted the general in mid-bite and
retrieved the cap.

A woman in Redlands, California, was at a lunch counter,
chatting with a middle-aged man beside her. "As we talked,"
she says, "my eyes kept straying to a piece of string hanging
down below his ear. Finally I couldn't stand it any longer,
and told him, 'You have a piece of string on your neck,'
and gave it a quick yank. Wow! I was staring, my face
poinsettia red, at his bald head. The 'string,' it seems, was
attached to the netting of his toupee and was supposed to
be tucked out of sight."

A lady in Columbus, Ohio, bought some sexy false eyelashes, but her nearsighted husband didn't even notice them.
Disappointed, she took them off and laid them on the
vanity table. The next morning she was awakened by a
terrible noise. There stood her husband with a newspaper,
banging away at her eyelashes. "What are you doing?" she
asked. "Stay back, honey!" he commanded. "I've killed one
of these things and I'm going to get the other one, too!"

One of the most enthusiastic, likable people in Hollywood
is Meredith Willson. Author of *The Music Man*, *The
Unsinkable Molly Brown*, and many other musical hits,

he is still the tousle-haired boy from Iowa, bright eyed and anxious to please. So it is with great sadness that I must report that on one occasion he deflated the ego of one of the town's Romeos and left a blossoming romance in the ash can. It all happened at the entrance to the Brown Derby when Meredith and his wife were leaving and met a famous producer and his much younger girl friend coming in. The producer was completely bald and was never seen without his beautifully made toupee. In fact, he had worn it so constantly and for so many years that Meredith, along with most of his other friends, had forgotten he *was* bald. So when the producer slapped Meredith on the shoulder and amid gay greetings commented on the wonderful head of hair the composer still had, it was only natural that Meredith would return the compliment. However, with his enthusi-

astic, boyish exuberance, words were not enough for Meredith. He cried, "Well, how about that great head of hair
that *you* still have!" And with that, he reached out and
grabbed a handful affectionately.

When the entire hairpiece came off in his hand the
laughter stopped, eyebrows raised, the producer gulped, the
girl shrieked, and Mr. and Mrs. Willson began talking
loudly and incoherently about the Dodgers, the weather,
the roast beef, and how well his necktie went with his
shoes. To this day, Meredith tells me, he will never know
how the hair got back on the producer's head, what they
really said, or how they got out the door and into their
car. Nature kindly provides a temporary amnesia at moments like this.

Movie insiders tell of the days when Marlon Brando was
shooting *Mutiny on the Bounty* on location in Tahiti. One
complex scene called for a bevy of native girls to dive from
the decks of the *Bounty* into the sea and swim ashore.
Since many of the island maidens aren't so gloriously en-
dowed as fiction would have us believe, the film's costume
designer padded out the extra girls with something extra—
American-style "falsies." As the cameras turned and Marlon
waved good-by to the *Bounty*'s bountiful maidens, they all
dived over the side—only to have their falsies boing up to
the surface. Falsies floated everywhere, bobbing on the
waves, and the girls were so tickled that they began playing
catch with them. Somehow this charming and spontaneous
action sequence was omitted from the final film. Obviously
Marlon Brando is no man to falsify a scene.

5

Havoc for Housewives

No housewife should ever answer the door, take a bath, greet a caller, go shopping, or so much as show her face outside the home. She should do none of these things, that is, if she is the least bit sensitive about awkward situations. My research has unearthed a rather startling contradiction. The housewife, long supposed to lead a routine and uneventful life, is actually beset with daily adventures and perils that would send Superman cowering back into his phone booth. Her day is crowded with narrow escapes and misadventures with neighbors, salesmen, repairmen, kids, and shopkeepers. Just to carry on in the front lines of housewifery, she must have the poise of a queen, the agility of a black-belt karate expert, and the patience of a man waiting to collect on a ninety-nine-year lease.

Consider the plight of a California lady who told me about taking her exercises in the nude in her upper-story apartment. She felt completely secure, since no one could see in. "I was sitting on the floor in my living room," she said, "doing a very difficult spread. When I raised up, I looked into the eyes of a telephone repairman at the very top of a pole. His expression and my own terror made me freeze

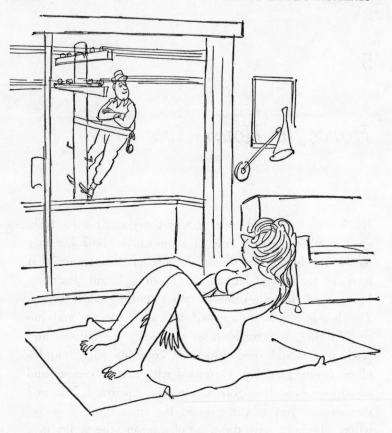

for a moment. And then, instead of getting up and running into the other room, I was so petrified that I crawled out on my hands and knees, got into bed, and covered up my head."

A lady who had been after her husband for months to install a garbage disposal under the kitchen sink finally trapped him one Saturday afternoon, and he glumly got to work with his wrenches. Not wishing to listen to his colorful vocabulary as he banged his thumbs, she went out shopping.

While downtown she ran into some girl friends and had a few cocktails, so she was feeling very friendly when she returned home. There was good old George still under the sink, working away, legs sticking out into the kitchen. So she bent down, reached under, and gave him a rudely familiar tweak. "Hi, honey," she said. There was a howl of surprise from under the sink as the man raised up and smacked his forehead against the disposal. It was the plumber! Her husband had given up on the job. The plumber crawled out, his forehead all bloody, and the wife ran to phone for an ambulance. The husband helped the attendant load the poor plumber onto a stretcher. "How'd it happen?" asked the attendant as they were carrying the man out. When the husband told him, the attendant began laughing so hard he let go of the stretcher—and the plumber plunged to the sidewalk, breaking his arm. Imagine explaining that one to the insurance company.

Another woman told me she'll never forget the morning she was doing the wash, when she heard someone coming down the steps. Thinking it was her little girl, who was ready for her nap, she said, "Get upstairs, honey, and get into bed. I'll be right there." Then she looked up—and it was the meter man.

A young mother said, "My four-year-old daughter found a sign and hung it on our front door. When a salesman came to the door, he just stood there laughing. I got mad and asked him, 'What's so funny?' He pointed to the sign. It said, 'Men at Work.'"

Anxious to make a good impression, the hostess for a ladies' group bought some four-dollar guest towels and put a note above them for her husband. It said, "If you use these towels, I'll kill you." The next day she enter-

tained the club women at luncheon. After the party she went into the bathroom. The note was still there—and the towels were untouched.

Have you ever had that typically feminine urge to take all your furniture and rearrange it, just to see how it would look? One housewife who had that nesting urge confessed to me that one day she had a wonderful time shifting around everything in the house. That night her husband returned to town on a late plane. Being a considerate sort, he decided to crawl into bed without turning on the lights so he wouldn't wake his darling mate. She woke up anyhow, and so did the neighbors, when he leaped into bed where the bed used to be. He struck the floor with a bone-jarring crash, then stumbled into lamps, chairs, and nightstands while groping for a light switch. We shall not pause to quote him on this incident, but there does appear to be a moral: Always be like Little Red Riding Hood and make sure it's safe before you jump into any beds.

Safety experts have long warned that most accidents happen in the home. Judging by my mail, I'd say the most dangerous appliance in any home is not the stove, a heater, or an iron—it's the front door. And here's proof:

A New Mexico woman told me this one: "I have a great big old boxer dog that I've had many years, and she's a regular pest sometimes. One day she was unusually persistent in wanting me to let her in and out. I let her out once more, and got into the bathtub. I had just gotten good and soapy when I heard her again. I threw a towel around me and yanked open the door yelling, 'Come in, you damned old fool!' I nearly fainted when I saw it was my minister smiling at me!"

After cleaning her house, a lady told her five-year-old son to watch for the insurance man while she was taking her bath. "Let me know the minute he arrives," she warned. She was in the tub when her son yelled, "Here he is, Mom!" The door opened, and there was Junior with a tall, shocked gentleman by the hand. The insurance man was obviously quite alarmed by her lack of coverage. In fact, he lost all assurance, turned his back on this risky prospect, and departed. Future payments on her policy were mailed to the home office.

Men love gadgets, and women love new appliances. One lady in Toledo, Ohio, told of the day her new washing machine arrived, and she couldn't wait to try it. Since she didn't have any dirty clothes to run through, she took off all her clothing and put it in the washer. Meanwhile her husband had gone out for groceries. Just as she got the washer going, she heard a sound at the door and said, "Bring them in, dear. I can't come to the door." As footsteps came down the basement stairs, she saw the shoes and realized that it was her bakery man, not her husband. "Wait a moment!" she yelled. "Stand right where you are." She turned off the machine, took her wet dress out, and put it on, getting her hair dripping wet in the process. Then she walked over to the bakery man, wringing wet. "What happened to you?" said the man. "I just got a new washing machine and was trying it out," she said. He gave her an odd look and said, "Lady—you're supposed to take off the dress before you put it into the washer."

Ordering her little boy to take his bath, a mother reminded him to leave his dirty clothes in the hallway. Moments later there was a soft knock on the door. Thinking it was her son, the mother opened it and said, "Come on in—and you'd better have your pants off!" It was her daughter's steady boy friend.

An Atchison, Kansas, woman heard on the radio that an escaped convict was in her neighborhood. The newscaster described him as being about six feet tall, balding, and a dangerous killer. She had the convict's description vividly in mind when a tall, bald man walked in the door without knocking. She began to scream as loud as she could. "Help! Police! He's a killer!" The man fled. When she'd gathered herself together, she stepped outside to spread the alarm, and found some bottles of milk on her porch. Her "killer" had been a substitute milkman.

Another lady tells of the day she applied a complexion

clay to her face and decided to read while it was working. The doorbell rang. "Who's there?" she said. "Delivery man," said the voice outside the door. She opened the door, the man took one horrified look at her masklike face, yelled, dropped the package, and ran down the stairs, two at a time.

No matter where you move in this land of ours, a parade of salesmen will soon beat a path to your door.

After moving into a new home, a woman in Detroit became weary of a succession of peddlers ringing her doorbell. When still another ring came, she yelled through the door, "I can't talk to you! I'm on a long-distance call." But the man kept leaning on her doorbell. Finally she threw open the door and began bawling him out. "I *told* you I was on the phone long distance," she said. "Why do you keep bothering me?" The man smiled and said softly, "Ma'am, I happen to be from the telephone company. I've come to *connect* your phone."

A Missouri wife of a police commissioner came in from a hot August day of shopping and stripped down to panties and bra for comfort. Just then a neighbor called and asked as a favor if she'd roll her hair, so she told the woman to come right over. Moments later the doorbell rang. "Come right in, I'm ready!" said she. In walked a policeman with a blue uniform, a red face, and a note from her husband.

Having two repairmen working in her house on the same day was almost the cause of a housewife falling apart. One man was there to fix the furnace, and the other to repair a broken commode. She was busy sewing and didn't bother to turn around when one of the men came in to announce that he was finished. Remembering that her husband wanted the furnace tested before the man left, she asked, "Did you try it out?" She was greeted by silence. Finally, with growing alarm, she turned around—to see a very shaken plumber.

Do you remember your first quarrel with your mate? How much it hurt when it happened—and how good it felt to make up? One young bride confessed to me that after three months of bliss she had her first serious quarrel with her husband and went to bed without kissing him good night. But she couldn't sleep, so she got up and wrote a passionate love note that she could slip into her husband's pocket for him to read before coming home. She also wrote a second message, a routine note to the milkman ordering butter, milk, and eggs. Imagine the wife's chagrin when her husband came home with the butter, milk, and eggs. The milkman had obviously gotten her love note—and it was a rather large order! P.S. The blushing bride changed milk companies at once.

Since it was a very important dinner party for her husband's new boss, another woman told me she had made some very grand hors d'oeuvres and set them out on a coffee table. A few minutes later she caught her dog gobbling them down as fast as he could. She put him outside and then began welcoming her guests. Her husband hadn't arrived yet because his plane was delayed. Everybody was enjoying cocktails and the remaining hors d'oeuvres for about an hour when a neighbor called over and said, "Your dog is lying dead in the alley." Horrified that her hors d'oeuvres might have been poisonous, she told the guests what had happened. The whole party raced in a convoy of cars to the hospital emergency room, had their stomachs pumped out, and then gamely returned to the party. When the lady's husband finally got home, his first words to his shaken guests were, "Our poor dog is lying crushed and dead out there in the alley. A hit-and-run driver must have got him."

What is so innocent as a new bride—in the kitchen? You've heard the jokes about new brides and their cooking, but these stories are really true:

A tearful bride asked an appliance salesman to come over immediately, because her refrigerator wasn't working properly and she was expecting guests. When he got there, she said, "I baked my first cake three hours ago and put it in the freezer, and there isn't even the slightest bit of frosting on it yet."

A bride whose husband told her how to fix a three-minute egg obediently put the egg in the water—along with the timer.

Another bride cooking at her mother-in-law's home served

up a dish of beautifully glazed onions—or so she thought. What she glazed and served were gladiola bulbs.

A dutiful bride packed lunches for her husband each day, always putting a fruit pie inside. After two weeks of this her husband said, "Please don't put any more pies in my lunch, darling." "Why not?" she asked. "Don't you like fruit pies?" "Yes," he said, "but I like them better cooked." She had been giving them to him frozen.

Another newlywed decided to bake some bread like her mother did, but it didn't rise. Not wanting her husband to know of her failure, she buried the bread in the garden. Later on, when the sun warmed the ground, she saw the bread rising right out of the earth. When her husband came home, there it was, poking out of the soil like a Martian mushroom.

If it's any consolation to brides, here is the story of a new husband who offered to help his wife in the kitchen. "I wasn't too good at piecrusts," she told me, "so I suggested he try his hand at that. I gave him a cookbook, some flour, shortening, and so forth, and let him go at it. Later on I looked over to see him swishing a fork through a bowl of water, aiming in the general direction of another bowl with flour and shortening in it. 'What on earth are you doing?' I said. 'Just exactly what it says in the cookbook,' said he. And he was right. The cookbook said, 'Add three tablespoons of water, tossing with a fork.'"

An Arizona woman tells of when she was first married: "I had a lot of time to experiment with cooking. I was never concerned about wasting food, because we had a large fifty-pound dog named Wrinkles that would eat anything that I cooked, preferring my bakery goods. Whenever I baked anything, she'd sit on a chair in the kitchen and drool. As soon as the cake or cookies cooled, I would always toss her several samples which she would catch in her mouth and gulp down.

"My Waterloo came the afternoon I decided to bake a perfect angel food cake. I followed the recipe to the letter and when the aroma of the oven filled the kitchen, Wrinkles got on the chair and drooled. Now, as you know, an angel food cake is usually about seven or eight inches high. After my cake had baked the allotted time it was barely one and a half inches high.

"Of course, when I removed it from the oven, Wrinkles danced around my feet, waiting for a piece of that delicious-smelling food. After it cooled, I 'chiseled' it out of the pan and was about to toss it into the garbage, but Wrinkles was so anxious that I tore a piece of it off and tossed it to her. She caught it in her mouth and immediately dropped it on the floor. Then she picked it up and ran to the door, dropped the cake again, and gave her usual bark that meant I should let her out. Then she picked up the cake and ran out while I stood in the doorway, curious to see what she would do. She put the cake down, dug a hole, dropped the cake into it, and covered it. Then she came back into the house wagging her tail as if to say, 'I've just buried another bone.'"

Here are some more kitchen catastrophes:

In a hurry while pressure-cooking a chicken, a housewife tried to release the steam with a fork. The fork slipped, and as she reported later, there was plenty of chicken to go around—all around the walls, the floor, and the ceiling.

A girl baking biscuits in cooking class misread her recipe. Instead of two cups of flour and a tablespoon of baking powder, she used a tablespoon of flour—and two cups of baking powder! By the time she realized her mistake, she was afraid to open the door. So was her teacher. Finally they did, and found she'd created something new—biscuits that went off like hand grenades.

A housewife put some dog food on a plate in the refrigerator. Naturally, when her husband came home, he made a sandwich with it. What hurt was his reaction: "Honey, this is the finest meat loaf you've ever made."

A Canoga Park, California, homemaker was doing what many a cook does, licking the beater while preparing some kitchen goodie. But her beater was electric, and she got her tongue caught in it. Hurt? No. Embarrassed? Yes.

By now it should be obvious that the true-life adventures of American housewives are at least as exciting as those of their favorite heroines in detergent dramas. It takes courage to stay home! But even if a housewife slips away on a shopping expedition, there's a whole new world of potentially disastrous moments waiting to entrap her. Shopping is like a safari: it's supposed to be fun, but there's a scent of the unexpected in the air, and anything can happen. Here are some things that *did* happen on shopping safaris:

Waiting patiently in line in a crowded department store, a woman couldn't help overhearing the man at the head of the line as he yelled and bellowed at the salesgirl. He ranted and raved, beating his fists on the counter. Aghast at this display of childish temper, she turned to a woman standing nearby and said, "Just listen to that big blubbering idiot, making a hundred dollars' worth of fuss over a dollar pair of socks. I'd sure hate to have him for a husband." The other woman glared at her and said, "He *is* my husband."

Another woman who was all tired out from a hard day's

shopping found herself being pushed to the rear of a crowded elevator. She happened to glance back over her shoulder and saw a small brown seat in the corner. She sank down on it to rest—and heard a piercing scream of protest. The "seat" was the head of a small boy wearing a tan beret!

A woman in Des Moines, Iowa, told me this one about window-shopping with her husband. "We saw a lovely bed-room set," she says, "so I said, 'How would you like to snuggle up in that lovely bed?' My husband said nothing, so I looked around. The man I was talking to was a stranger."

While a friend was paying a department-store bill, a woman who came along with her sank down into a lounge

chair for a rest. As she was leaving, a man came up. "Excuse me," he said, "but there's something stuck on the back of your coat." He was smiling, and she soon found out why: she had sat down on a price tag and her posterior was plainly labeled "Bargain price—$6.95."

An expectant mother was shopping in a grocery store with her husband. She left him with the cart and then returned, throwing her arms around him for a kiss. It was bad enough that the man wasn't her husband, but when his wife walked up glaring, at this expectant woman she didn't know—ouch!

Another woman who was expecting her baby soon made frequent trips to a grocery store that was just around the corner. She was mystified why the clerk seemed to think her condition was so amusing. Then one day she saw herself in the mirror and realized what he was laughing at. Printed across the front of her flour sack apron which she always wore shopping were the words "Self-rising."

Returning to her car laden with groceries, a woman was frustrated to find the car door locked and stuck. The parking attendant tried several keys and then agreed when she insisted to break her door handle with a crowbar. After getting inside the car, the woman discovered it wasn't hers! She waited for the rightful owner and offered to repay him for the damage, but he refused. "I own a garage," he said, "and I can fix it. Besides, I'm happy to find somebody else has a wife as dumb as mine is."

Most women love to window-shop, and most men don't. I suspect this is because women like to dream of what they would buy if they could, whereas a man lacks the courage it takes to look one salesman after another in the eye and with absolutely no intention of buying anything. One woman told me of window-shopping an entire jewelry store, fondling the rings, necklaces, and bracelets, and then going on her way without buying so much as a bead. After the exhilarating experience of being up to her elbows in diamonds and pearls, she crossed the street to a department store, leaned on a cosmetics counter—and three expensive pieces of jewelry slid out of her coat sleeve! Obviously her sleeve had scooped them up without her realizing it, and had "shoplifted" the merchandise. She gathered up the gems and swept them into her handbag while a very suspicious clerk gave her a policewoman's eye. Then the lady raced back to the jewelry store, "confessed," and went home to enjoy a quiet panic.

When inexpensive wigs were a big fad, a mother took her four-year-old son to a discount store. The boy saw a woman walking down the aisle wearing one of the wigs uncombed, and he yelled, "Oh, Mommy! Look! Yogi Bear!"

After baking several loaves of bread, a Cincinnati housewife told me, she ran out of wax paper. She went to the store, but the clerk misunderstood her request and brought her a roll of bathroom tissue. Noticing only the width of it, she asked, "Is that the widest you've got?" The clerk said, "Well, lady, what do you want to use it for?"

Often it isn't what you say but how you say it. A woman shopping in a fashionable store in Dallas was about to make a purchase in the bedding department. Deep in thought, she looked up at the clerk and said in a loud voice, "Are you sure it's safe to sleep with my husband under an electric blanket?" Before the clerk could answer this delicate question, the woman turned crimson, dropped the blanket as though it were high voltage, and headed for the nearest exit.

Some of the greatest embarrassing moments are like ava-

lanches. They start with just the smallest trickle of dis-
comfiture, and then there's a crack in the façade of human
dignity, and finally the entire personality collapses in dust
and ruin. Those are the funniest of all, because they are
cumulative. One of them I heard about happened quite
recently near San Francisco. A woman was driving along in
her car with five children. One of them had a little pet
lizard, and he put it on his mother's shoulder. Suddenly the
lizard ran down into her brassiere! She screamed and pulled
over to the side of the road, jumped out of the car, and
started wiggling her body while in a bent position to see if
she couldn't shake it out. Another motorist coming along
saw her in these strange contortions and, thinking she had
a seizure, stopped his car, jumped out, ran over, threw her
down, and started pulling her tongue out of her mouth! A
second man who was walking by thought that the first man
was attacking the woman, so he got a club and hit the first
man over the head, knocking him out. At this, the woman
got up and gasped, "I was just trying to get a lizard out of
my brizzard." Can you imagine the good Samaritan's expression as he stood over the prostrate man with a club in
his hand?

Another story that started innocently and just kept ava-
lanching happened to a lady who writes, "I called my doctor
to send over one of his precious prescriptions so a friend of
mine who had an inflamed throat wouldn't have to pay for
a visit to a physician. I let my doctor think it was *my*
throat that was sore, and he insisted that I come to his office
immediately. 'But, Doctor,' I said. 'No buts,' said the doctor.
'Come right down here.' I had to. Before going, I colored
my throat with little red candies. The doctor took one look

at my throat, then swabbed it with medicine, gave me a shot in the hip with the longest needle I'd ever seen, took my temperature, and then sat me down and gave me a long lecture: 'You must lose weight, and I want you to report to my office every week for three months. Start with these diet pills.' I got the original prescription I went after for my friend—but oh, that doctor bill!"

A lady attending a family barbecue had nicked her finger while carving, so she walked into the bathroom for a Band-Aid. She unwittingly surprised her brother-in-law stepping out of the tub, so she retreated and rejoined the family. Meanwhile her brother-in-law's wife wanted to show her their new bedspread, so into the bedroom they went—and encountered the same man, who had just come in from the tub and was *still* unclad. After two of these confrontations the lady ran back out to the living room for a moment to compose herself. Then she remembered she still hadn't gotten that Band-Aid. Back she went to the bathroom, just in time to surprise her *other* brother-in-law *in flagrante*. (Editor's note: *In flagrante* is a Latin expression for "oops.")

In this chapter we have seen our heroine, the housewife, manning her doorbell and bathtub against all comers and frightening off such luckless intruders as plumbers, milkmen, and bashful insurance agents. We have looked beneath the seemingly placid surface of the average household and found that "safe at home" is an expression suitable only for baseball.

Next we will see how modern life with all its gadgets has created whole new kinds of embarrassments, ways to lose face and redden cheeks that never existed before. You will also read one of my favorite boo-boos of the century which has never been told before, to my knowledge, because it happened to a super-secret group of scientists working on development of the first atomic bomb. It seems their first big shipment of plutonium had arrived and . . . well, I'll tell you later.

6

Boo-boos and Dum-dums

Modern life with its treacherous gadgetry has brought us hundreds of new ways to embarrass ourselves. It's not surprising when you stop to think that every invention to make life easier also makes it more complicated. Consider the woman visiting a new supermarket who marvels when an automatic door opens at her approach. But as she pauses in reverence at this mechanical miracle, the same door whacks her across the backside when another shopper comes through. A man watches a movie from his car at a local drive-in and then heads for home—only to hear a tremendous crash. The movie loudspeaker is still inside his window, and he has pulled it out by its electronic roots. A young mother enjoys the convenience and informality of feeding the kids at a drive-in restaurant. But then they turn the radio on too loud, so she hurriedly rolls up the car window—and the dishes on the window tray go smashing in all directions. A minister pauses for a bite at a busy hamburger stand and reaches for one of the new plastic bottles of mustard. The bottle refuses to pour until he gives it a mighty squeeze. Then it suddenly lets go, baptizing the other customers. That's how life is in America the Technical, with a new

way to get in trouble for every way to do something better.

It is now notorious that electronics technicians who care for such skulduggery can turn any man's castle into a fishbowl by wiring the rooms with tiny transmitters. In fact, a whole building full of apartment dwellers blushed simultaneously recently when they learned of their landlord's "hobby"—listening in on his private network of microphones in their bedrooms! Each night he would tune around from one bedroom to another until he found a Late Late Show to his liking. No one would ever have known if he hadn't been exposed accidentally, and it's quite possible that other gadget-minded characters have since followed his naughty example. (And where is *your* landlord tonight?)

Another modern marvel is direct distance dialing. With a handful of the right numbers, you can be talking in seconds to Saskatchewan, Canada—and so can your babysitter. Like many another technical triumph, direct distance dialing works just fine; it's the people who use it who get mixed up. A lady in Chicago told me of wanting to surprise her sister in Florida with a birthday phone call. They hadn't seen each other for years, although they wrote regularly. She got out her address book and dialed. No answer. She dialed again and again, all evening long, until in sheer exasperation she decided to go the old-fashioned route and call the operator. "I'll be happy to try the number for you," said the voice with a smile. "What is it?" The caller told her. There was a long pause, and then the operator said, "That is not a telephone number, madam. It is a zip code."

Generally an embarrassing moment happens to one person. Occasionally two or three are caught up in the same faux pas. But rarely has an entire staff of eminent scientists acquired a collective red face as they did in an incredible incident that may well go down in history as the boo-boo of the twentieth century. It involved our biggest wartime secret, the Manhattan Project, which was attempting to produce the first atomic weapon. The time was early in 1942, and the place was the University of Chicago. Plutonium was the necessary material, and almost none of it had ever been collected. At the cost of millions, a plant to produce it had finally been constructed on the West Coast in a race against the Nazis, who were known to be conducting similar experiments. At last the first two precious beakers of plutonium were delivered in utmost secrecy to the Chicago group of physicists. The entire staff was notified to meet promptly the next morning to discuss how best to use the invaluable stuff in various experiments.

That night, so I'm told by a veteran of the Chicago group, a diligent janitor came through the guards and locked doors with all the proper clearances to tidy up the laboratory. He dusted, rearranged chairs, scrubbed sinks, and poured down the drain the contents of two beakers that sat in the midst of this highly classified inner sanctum.

The next morning a popeyed director announced to a horrified staff that the plutonium was gone—down the drain, into the sewers of Chicago! The janitor was detained for questioning while the scientists summoned Chicago sanitation experts to rush over with maps of the sewers—without telling them why. The main one from the lab was hastily closed off. Then technicians began following the line down the street for about two and a half blocks, where the radioactive material was trapped in a sluggish stream.

Now these top-level experts, the world's finest brains, began carrying buckets of sewage back to the laboratory for the delicate task of extracting the precious plutonium. To the relief of the responsible officials, the incident was kept quiet, and the radioactive material was all recovered. The scientists showered, soaped, showered again, then gathered to discuss the next problem: what to do with the shovels, pails, and other gear that had been used and were contaminated by the plutonium. This was their first experience with the problem of what to do with radioactive waste materials that would have a half life of twenty-five thousand years!

The Geiger-sensitive junk was lying in a small pile in the heavily guarded yard outside the lab while the big brains struggled with the question of how to dispose of it. Meanwhile a junkman arrived, piled everything in his truck, and drove out to the city dump where he piled it on several tons of other junk from that day's collection.

Later that afternoon a scientist came dashing in with news of the latest disaster. The junkman was now detained for questioning while the harassed brain trust put on their decontamination gear and went out to find the newly contaminated junk. Hours later they brought back and piled up in the yard a mountain of old tires, mattresses, bottles, cartons, and, of course, the original shovels and pails that caused all the trouble.

Now a special guard was placed over the junk heap, and an emergency meeting to end all emergency meetings was called. The badly rattled scientists discussed dozens of ideas for getting rid of the radioactive rubbish, but no one had a suggestion that didn't involve a risk.

At last the meeting door opened and the officer in charge of the guard reported. The United States Army had sent over a detachment of soldiers with a large-scoop steam shovel. They scooped up the whole mess and drove out of the yard and the lives of the scientists. To this day, as my

informant tells it, they have never learned where the junk
went or what was done to it. And they have never asked.

Those situation comedies that you and I watch on television couldn't possibly be funnier than the incredible hap-
penings of daily life. We think it's pure slapstick when we
see someone like Lucille Ball walking down the street and
suddenly disappearing into an open manhole; and yet that
really happened to a housewife in Iowa. Even more unlikely
was the experience of a Los Angeles woman who was walking along the sidewalk when a pigeon gently alighted on her
hair—and laid an egg! Another scene worthy of a comedy
happened during World War II, when off-duty sailors frequently slept in their gun turrets. One day in port, according

to an ex-swabbie who saw it happen, a sailor awoke in his turret, unaware that the turret door had been turned seaward during the night. Half asleep, he clambered out— and dropped right over the side into the ocean.

An official representing a prominent service club in the Midwest was awarding achievement medals to some ladies in a local community group. As each lady came on stage, he pinned on her medal. He was doing fine until one ample-bosom matron appeared. The jab of the pin brought a tell-tale hiss of air, and he watched in shock as her bosom deflated. Then he rushed through the rest of the ceremony and got out of there, feeling rather deflated himself.

After watching a movie a Florida woman emerged in the lobby and was startled to find an odd furry object dangling from her blouse button. Just then a man who'd been sitting in front of her came dashing out, bald as an egg. She had snagged his hairpiece and scalped him.

Have you ever found yourself doing the exact thing you wanted most to avoid? You go over and over what you *don't* want to do in your mind, until it's rehearsed so perfectly that you're sure to do it. Newlyweds are often victims of this reverse mechanism, in their understandable desire to avoid attention by trying to look very cool and old-married on their honeymoons. One such bridegroom sauntered casually up to a hotel clerk, signed "Mr. and Mrs." as though he had done it for years, and then sent the clerk falling off his chair with this line: "I'd like a double bed with a room, please."

Another groom who dreaded being stared at cautioned his bride again and again to behave as if they had been married for years. They had even avoided signing into the bridal suite, so no one would know they were honeymooners. The next morning the couple went down to the hotel dining room for their first breakfast together. The waitress brought coffee and asked for their orders. The bride looked up and said, "Nothing else, thank you. The coffee will be fine." The groom, a staunch believer in starting the day with a good meal, looked up in shock and forgot himself for one awful moment. "Good Lord, woman," his voice boomed through the dining room, "is coffee all you ever have for breakfast?"

A couple traveling West on the first night of their honeymoon were discouraged by "No Vacancy" signs until they reached a rural ranch area with a sign that said, "Tourists Welcome." Wearily they signed in and dragged themselves to their honeymoon suite. The bridegroom snapped on the lights, and they found that their "suite" was a ranch house with six sets of bunk beds! (I think they spent the rest of the night in tiers.)

One marital mixup I'll never forget happened when I was in New York for several TV appearances. One of my best friends, Allen Chase, was being married on the West Coast at the same time, and he wanted me to give away the bride because her mother and father couldn't be there. So I flew all the way back to Hollywood from New York, rushed into the house, and joined the wedding procession. Another old friend, Dr. James A. Peterson, was conducting the marriage ceremony as he has hundreds of others, including that of my son, Jack. I stood there waiting, mentally going over my traditional line, something like "In the absence of her father, I give this woman." Suddenly I realized something was wrong. Dr. Peterson was concluding the ceremonies, and the ring was being put on! I had that nightmarish

feeling that every actor has had, wondering if I'd been thinking about something else and missed my cue.

Had I been daydreaming, and did they go right by me?
So after the ceremony I went to Dr. Peterson and asked,
"What happened?" A look of pained dismay and utter shock
spread over his face. "I forgot about you," he said. "I've
never done this before in my whole life." Here I had
crossed the entire continent, from coast to coast, to say *one*
line—and never got a chance to say it. All I could do was
shrug my shoulders, grin at my embarrassed friend the minister, and catch the next plane back to New York for
. . . "What's My Line."

Have you ever wanted to clobber one of those obnoxious
characters, male or female, who push and elbow their way
past you? A newspaper cameraman that I know got his
revenge when one of these all-American shovers, a hefty
woman shopper, got into a crowded express elevator in the
Los Angeles City Hall and bulldozed her way to the rear
of the car. As she swung around to face the front, she
plastered my friend into the corner and scrunched down on
his toes as well. That was too much. Bang! The big flash-
bulb on his press camera went off with a blinding glare.
The woman howled as the hot bulb singed right through
her girdle. Passengers gasped, thinking the elevator had
shorted out. The operator froze at the controls, letting the
car plunge several floors before he brought it to a stop. When
the woman got enough of her breath back to speak, she
demanded to know what had happened. My friend smiled
and pointed to his flashgun. "I'm awful sorry, lady," he
said. "You backed right into this little red button."

Here are some more real-life boo-boos and dum-dums:
A lady from White Plains, New York, told me she was

making such marvelous progress in her yoga lessons that she tried to see if she could put her leg behind her head. Slowly, carefully, she lifted her heel up, and up—and she made it! Smiling in triumph, she began to pull her leg free again— but it wouldn't come. She tugged but couldn't get unstuck. "Help!" she yelled, and her husband dashed in to de-pretzel-ize her.

A Boston woman thought it would be fun to dye her hair green for St. Patrick's Day, so she did. She was the loveliest colleen of them all that day, if you like green hair, and she had a wonderful time. The next morning she be-gan rinsing her hair before going to work—and the green wouldn't come out. She scrubbed and scrubbed, but the green stayed green. So she went to work, green-haired and red-faced. She looked like an Irish mermaid for several days, until a beauty operator concocted a supersolution that re-moved the green at last.

Two teen-age girls whose dates took them to a roller-skating rink for the first time went wobbling bravely across the rink—and rolled right into the men's rest room! There they stayed helplessly, too excited and embarrassed to ma-neuver back out again, until their boy friends came skating to the rescue.

A woman opening a new charge account was asked what her husband did for a living. "He's a policeman," she said. And then, thinking it might be helpful if the credit manager knew her husband had other income from part-time jobs, she asked, "Do you want to know what he makes on the side?"

A milk truck tipped over at a corner in Phoenix, Arizona. A crowd gathered to stare at the hundreds of bottles smashed all over the street, with milk running in the gutters. A man

in the crowd who was peering over the shoulders of a very plump woman said, "Oh boy, what a waste." The woman whirled around indignantly and said, "I'll ask you to mind your own business!"

A lady I know tells what a shattering experience it was to ride a New York subway during the rush hour for the first time. She was caught up in the crowd that surged into the car just as the doors slammed shut, catching her fox scarf. "Stop the car!" she yelled. "I've lost my tail!"

A man in Lincoln, Nebraska, was accustomed to making one of those split-second dashes out the door for the bus each morning. One day, after he had sprinted down the street, his wife noticed that his lunch pail was still sitting on the stove. She grabbed it and dashed up the street, meeting her rosy-faced husband who was standing there—with her teakettle in his hand.

Have you ever been so busy that you ran off in all directions at once? I can still picture the Denver lady who told me she thought she had survived the seasonal madness of the Christmas rush—until she looked in the bathroom mirror and found she was taking a bath with her hat on.

Unable to sleep, a Houston, Texas, woman got a prescription for sleeping pills from her doctor. He told her to take two at bedtime. "I slept quite soundly that night," she says, "but I sure was puzzled when I woke up to see that my two sleeping pills were still on the nightstand. I was sure I swallowed them. Then I remembered that I had promised to sew two buttons on my husband's shirt—and the buttons were gone."

Another woman in Palm Beach, Florida, told me of the day she was resting on a bench at a flower show when a strange woman sat down beside her and said she had a headache. "I have some aspirin," she said, and gave the lady two tablets. The woman was very thankful. After she left, our good Samaritan looked in her bag. The aspirin were still there. She had given the woman two tablets from a bottle she had just bought at the show for her plants at home—a bottle of fertilizer tablets!

Sometimes we make boo-boos and have no idea for weeks or years that anything is amiss. One of those delayed-action stories was told to me by an Ohio lady. "I like antique

sales," she said, "so I went to one and bought some old jars and vases. One of them was particularly dirty, so I soaked and scrubbed it thoroughly. Afterward it was so lovely that I put it atop the organ. One afternoon a neighbor was admiring it. I told her I thought it was a beautiful old vase. She looked sweetly at me and said, 'It *is* nice—but whose ashes are in it?'"

If you have ever had a flat tire on a cold and rainy night, you can sympathize with a Chicago man who told me an experience that sounds like a Danny Thomas story. The tire blew out on a pitch-black country road, with the rain coming down in freezing gusts. Without an umbrella or raincoat, my friend stepped into the downpour to get his jack out of the trunk. His flashlight was gone. Somehow he managed to fumble the jack into position, unable to see a thing, got the car jacked up, and changed the tire. His hands were skinned and numb with cold, but at last the job was done. With chattering teeth, he crawled back in the car, stepped on the gas—and heard an ominously familiar "thump, thump, thump"! He crawled back out to check the trouble, and I shall spare you his exact words as he saw that he had changed the wrong tire.

While visiting her father at the hospital, a lady whose dog was to have puppies that day called home to see what was happening. She was so excited to hear the dog was having a large litter, she told me, that she came running into the hospital lobby and yelled to the rest of the family, "She's had eight and there are more coming!" Heads swiveled around from all directions, and faces registered shocked disbelief. People were muttering, "Eight? Did she say eight?" and others were saying, "Yes! And more coming!" She was so flustered when she realized what the strangers were thinking that she announced, "I have to go back now —to see how Daddy is doing."

It was an exciting moment for the young mother and her firstborn baby as they were bundled up and made ready for the trip home. The father arrived, helped his wife into the car, and off they went. Halfway home he turned the car around. "What's the matter, dear?" said his wife. "We forgot something," he said. "The baby."

Visiting hours at the hospital that night were over, but

a Detroit woman told me she was determined to see her daughter anyhow—so she sneaked in. After looking around to make sure nobody saw her, she pressed the button for the elevator—and doctors and nurses came running from all directions. Her "elevator" button was the fire alarm.

A young mother told me of the day she was registering her baby at a clinic. "What is your church affiliation?" the clerk asked. "Catholic," said mother. "Name of father?" said the clerk. "There are four of them," mother replied. The clerk put down her pencil and stared up at her, eyebrows raised. "Four of them?" The mother reddened. "Oh, this baby has only one father," she said. "He's my husband." The eyebrows rose farther and the mother stumbled onward, saying, "The other four fathers are at the church. It's a very big church, and, well, hmmm . . ."

When beer was illegal during Prohibition, a Denver family followed the national custom of making home brew in the basement. To avoid embarrassment with their nondrinking neighbors, the mother told the children to say it was "the cat prowling around" whenever a bottle blew its top, as often happened. One day while the teetotaling neighbors were calling on them, a bottle in the basement let go, and one of the kids said, "Hey, Mom! Another cat just blew up!"

A man in Dania, Florida, who was invited to a Halloween masquerade party decided to go as a woman. He gave himself the full Cinderella treatment—putting on a blonde wig, lipstick, eyeshadow, and a fetching dress. He even shaved his legs and put nail polish on his toes. It was all worth the effort, because everybody at the party thought he was a living doll. After the party broke up in the early hours, he went home—and became very ill. Next thing he knew, he was being rushed to the hospital in an ambulance for

an emergency operation. After the first confusion among
attendants about who or what he was, he underwent surgery. Then followed seventeen humiliating days, with every
doctor and nurse in the entire hospital finding time to peek
in at Halloween Henry.

A woman and her teen-age son were traveling through
Texas and decided to stop off in a small town to call on a
cousin. Nobody was home but the door was open, so they
went in to wait. The woman's feet were hurting, so she
went into the bathroom and soaked them in hot water.
Meanwhile her son raided the refrigerator and settled down
in the living room to watch TV. After waiting an hour or
so, the woman told her son to telephone their cousin's
office and see when he or his wife would be home. That's
how they learned their cousin had quit and left town three
months before. The visitors also left town—immediately.

Do you remember the days of the rubber bathing suit?
An Indiana woman recalls a beautiful yellow one that she
wore on a swimming outing with friends. After a cooling
dip she sat on a warm rock. She watched the others having
fun, unaware that the hot sun was slowly vulcanizing her
suit to the rock. "Come on in!" someone yelled. "Okay," she
said. "Here I come!" She leaped to her feet, and r-r-r-rip!
The southern end of her suit came off! She kept right on
going for the water, and that's where she put her clothes
back on.

After years of dreaming and plans for building a new
home, a couple in Tulsa, Oklahoma, bought a lot and set
to work. The husband was his own contractor, carpenter,
and everything else the building code would allow. After
finishing the basement and the framing, he went downtown
to get plumbing permits. The city clerk checked the records

and said, "I think you gave me the wrong address." "No, I didn't," said our friend. "That's my own home and I ought to know where I'm going to live." Together they looked at a map and found he was building on the wrong lot. In fact, his new home straddled two lots owned by different people. Fortunately both lot owners were willing to sell, so he didn't have to pull down the walls and start over. Besides— how do you move a basement?

A man in Laguna Hills, California, has good reason to remember the day he first registered to vote. The officials

asked for proof that his Polish-born father was a naturalized American, so he went home for the papers. Unfortunately his dad, in the first joyous flush of winning his citizenship, had nailed his papers on the door for his sons to see. Time had now literally glued the old documents to the door. Rather than risk damaging the papers, he and his brothers removed the door from its hinges, carried it down five flights of stairs, and showed it to the officials. Fortunately the board did not see fit to keep the door for their files, and returned it.

A woman who's a pet lover like myself tells me she was delighted to get a handsome Irish setter puppy for her birthday. But as he grew bigger and bigger (by leaps and bounds, of course) she was dismayed to find her apartment growing smaller and smaller. "Don't worry," her friends assured her. "He'll be no problem at all if you have him trained for obedience. It's easy—you can do it yourself." She accepted this advice and checked out a book on dog training at the library. The book is now overdue. The dog ate it.

The daughter of a nearsighted gentleman told me this story about her dad, who faithfully watered a particularly lovely plant that his wife had brought home several months before. Then one day he bent down to see how the plant was doing. It was artificial.

Two policemen in a squad car sped off to an apartment on a hot tip that a very dangerous bank bandit was holed up there. They dashed up the stairs, guns drawn, burst through the door and yelled, "Get your hands up!" at the man, who whirled around as they came charging in. Instead of raising his hands, the man fainted. He was just a traveling salesman. The bandit lived on the next floor up.

A good Samaritan told me this one on himself:

He saw a woman slide and fall on an icy sidewalk, so he hastened to help her. Just as he reached her, he lost his balance and landed smack on top of her. She sat up and said, "Watch where you're going, you clumsy oaf!"—and fetched him a roundhouse blow with her purse that rattled his teeth. Moral: Beware of fallen women.

A St. Louis woman had just completed a Red Cross course and was walking down the street one day when she saw a man lying face down in a flooded gutter. She raced to his aid, turned him over on his back, lifted his neck high, and began giving him mouth-to-mouth respiration. He sat up, pushing her away, and said, "What do you think you're doing, lady? I'm trying to fix this drain!"

During years of playing games and doing stunts with contestants on various shows, I found that I could count on the average person to do almost anything to maintain his dignity. No matter how absurd a situation became, he would go right on making the fatal mistake of pretending that everything was all right. Naturally this instinct to save face at all costs has created some of our most hilarious moments; and in the next chapter you'll see what happens when dignity goes riding on a skateboard.

7

"Oops!"

If I had been Diogenes, looking for an honest man, I would have searched for a real old-timer with a long gray beard. Older people don't care nearly so much as the rest of us about what others think, and they'll tell you the truth. So will kids, because they're born honest and haven't learned yet to tell those little white lies that grownups find so necessary in life. In between these truth-sayers, the very young and the very old, are the rest of us humans, all on our best behavior, being polite and dignified, and constantly concerned with making a good impression on everybody else. So if I were asked what are the most embarrassing moments in all of life, I'd say they come when we're caught with our pretenses down. We're trying to maintain our dignity under impossible conditions and wind up looking silly and foolish.

I think the late James Thurber, with his genius for appreciating absurd human predicaments, would have loved a story like this one that was told by a woman on my "House Party" show on CBS: She and her husband were driving to a party, and she was feeling a little uncomfortable because she was expecting a baby in just two months. So when they arrived at the place where the party was going on, she told her husband, "You go in by yourself, honey, and say you had to leave me home. I'll just sit out here in the car until you say your good-bys." He agreed and went inside. A few moments later the front door opened again and she heard someone say, "Oh, you have your new car. Let's see it." Footsteps came closer and closer. Trying desperately to hide, she scrunched herself down on the car floor. She could hear her husband gamely trying to steer the determined sightseers away, but it was no use. The host and hostess opened the car door, and there she was, seven months pregnant, tucked up into a ball—and speechless.

All of us know a Mr. and Mrs. Dullbore, people we dread to see but simply can't seem to avoid. So we can sympathize with a young couple who decided not to answer the door one Sunday when they spied some very boring acquaintances driving up outside. Since the apartment was small, the couple realized their visitors would see them unless they hid somewhere, so they crawled behind the sofa. The doorbell rang and rang. With stubborn persistence the callers leaned on the bell for several minutes. At last they walked off, and the couple popped out of hiding. But soon they heard more footsteps, so they dived behind the sofa again. The bell rang on and on. Then came the unmistakable sound of a key turning in the lock. The door swung open and they heard Mr. and Mrs. Dullbore saying, "Maybe something terrible has happened to them. We saw their car on the street and we can't understand where they could be." "Well, if you're that worried," replied the landlady's voice, "we'll look around a bit." They did, and they found them—on their knees, looking up from behind the sofa.

Judging by my mail, it's very common for women to go
dashing about outside the home in naught but a nightie,
thinking nothing will happen. Quite often they are spec-
tacularly overoptimistic, like the woman who was wearing a
filmy negligee when she drove off to get her teen-age daughter at a theater that let out at midnight. Halfway there,
her car sputtered and quit, out of gas. Knowing she could

get help at a twenty-four-hour service station a few blocks away, she slipped out of the car and cautiously began flitting from one tree to another, like a shy wood nymph. Just then a police car came cruising by and she yelled, "Wait! I need some help." The officers slammed on the brakes, she stepped out from behind her tree, and the squad car's searchlight swung around and caught her. There she stood, trapped in the glare of a powerful beam that lit her up like a stripper at a burlesque show. "Turn that off!" she pleaded. The officers, after studying the situation very carefully, flicked off the spotlight and drove away to get her some gas. Meanwhile she sprinted back to her car and just sat there, blushing brightly in the dark.

Another woman who had been sitting up late, addressing envelopes for her husband, gathered up the mail and drove to the post office without bothering to put anything on over her nightgown. She looked around very carefully when she got there, making absolutely sure that there wasn't another soul on the streets to see her. Then she leaped out and began jamming envelopes into the letter box. At that instant she heard a long, low, lecherous whistle. Yelping in fright, she dashed back into the car, falling all over herself. Then she discovered that the long, low whistle had come from her own car radio.

Another lady told me that she slipped out the front door at dawn to let her cat out, and the wind blew the door shut. Freezing cold in her skimpy "baby doll" outfit, she ran across the street to ask the neighborhood handyman to pry her door open. This kindly character agreed to help her, and loaned her one of his jackets to keep warm while he worked on her door. When he'd finished and she was safely inside again, she handed him back his jacket and thanked him for coming over. Just then she glanced next door and saw the curtains were parted. And there were the eyes of the neighborhood gossip, taking in the scene!

Less embarrassing but thoroughly ridiculous was the situation of a woman who was about ready to drop off to sleep when she realized she hadn't fed her dog. Sleepily she wandered into the kitchen in her nightie, fixed a dish of food, and took it outside to the doghouse. At that instant her neighbor's floodlights snapped on, lighting up the entire yard—and her. A late party was just getting started, and guests were already coming down the walk through her yard. With no time to sprint for the house, she dived into the doghouse beside her astonished pet and kept him company for an hour until the parade of guests was over.

Sometimes all it takes to create a real sizzler of an awkward moment is to be doing something perfectly ordinary and have someone misunderstand your actions. That's what happened to two sweet little old ladies who were sitting on a bench on a college campus one pleasant afternoon. There was a statue before them of the school's founder, and one of the ladies became curious about it. Just as she peeked under the statue's coat to see if it was hollow, an undergraduate came by, wagged his finger, and said, "Naughty, naughty!"

You might think that movie stars and other celebrities would be practically immune to embarrassments, because they're so used to appearing in public—but if you believe that, you're underestimating what the public can do to a performer's self-esteem. At Hollywood premieres, for example, it's traditional for stars to arrive in limousines that cruise slowly by the fans that are lining the streets. When your car reaches the entrance, someone on the public address system announces your arrival. But long before you can get to the theater, people will poke their heads in the window and say something such as, "Are you anybody?" Or they'll look in, eye everyone inside very carefully, and then say, "Is there anybody in here?" One experience like that can get a star's ego back down to size in a tremendous hurry!

One of our most beautiful nightclub stars, Marguerite Piazza, told me what happened to her at her opening engagement in the plush Cotillion Room of New York's Pierre Hotel. Her new nightclub act was an elaborate production which was unique to show business, because it featured several costume changes right on stage, inside a silken screen held up by poles. Her head and legs could be seen as she changed, unzipping one dress and tossing it over to a dancer who brought her the next costume. But this time she'd just flung her dress over the top of the screen as a dancer bumped into one of the poles—and the silk, like the walls of Jericho, came a-tumbling down. There she stood, clad only in a brief nude-colored undergarment— which made her look as if she was wearing nothing whatever. But Marguerite clung to her poise, even though there was nothing much else to cling to. She gathered up the fallen silk and draped it around her, Indian-sari style, waited calmly while the dancers scrambled to put her dressing tent up again, and then went on with the show.

One of the most popular actors in Hollywood, Emmy Award-winning Cliff Robertson, tells this one on himself: He was on location at the enormous Los Angeles International Airport, playing the role of an airline pilot who had to run down the long corridors to his plane. After five "takes," poor Cliff was ready to drop with exhaustion, so he headed for the airport cocktail lounge to collect himself. He was enjoying a leisurely martini when a flustered public relations man from the airline whose uniform Cliff was wearing came over and said, "Would you please leave here, sir? They think you're one of our pilots!" In fact, the ticket counter had already had three cancellations since Cliff appeared in the bar!

I have a lot to do with theaters in the round, and these have spawned a whole new series of embarrassing moments because the audience almost participates in the theatrical performance. It sees all the scenery moved up and down the aisles and the actors running in to get onto the circular stage in the center of the two- to three-thousand-seat theater. Everyone is cautioned in advance of each performance to stay out of the aisles or he may be run over by eager performers or stagehands with sets and scenery.

One man was unable to remember this admonition because of an even more urgent call, the call of nature, which began to plague him midway in the first act of the musical *Finian's Rainbow*. It was a moment when one actor in the center of the stage said, "Oh God, make me black." At this point the lights were to be turned out and the actor was to run up the aisle where two dressers and a makeup man were waiting for him in the darkness to prepare him for his next scene, in which he would be a Negro. The moment the blackout came, our man in the audience dashed for the men's room, only to be seized at the top of the aisle, turned around, his coat taken off and black makeup smeared all over his face. When the lights came on he was being pushed down onto the stage!

Another mixup came at an opening of *The Sound of Music*. If you've seen this show presented in the round,

you know it begins with a very beautiful procession of nuns making their way down the aisle, singing as they come down toward the stage. On this particular night it happened that a group of real nuns had come to see the show. They were a little late and were standing at the head of an aisle, waiting to be ushered down. Just then the stage manager came by and gave a couple of them a sharp rap on the bottom with a gentle admonition, "All right, girls, shake it up, and make it good!"

You might think I have a readily recognizable face, but

I'm frequently mistaken for someone else. Most of the time it's Ralph Edwards; occasionally it's been Jack Benny. But one of my dizziest experiences came the other night when a man approached me at a large formal party and said, "You may not remember me but I'll never forget you. My wife and I danced to your orchestra down at the Venice pier many years ago when we were courting." I said in some bewilderment, "You don't know who I am, do you?" He said, "Yes. You're Art Linkletter. I'll never forget you and your big band and those great romantic numbers you used to play." So he knew who I was, and yet he didn't—because he was calling me by my real name but remembering the champagne music of Lawrence Welk.

Sometimes strangers get you so involved in what they're saying that you find yourself going along with a completely ridiculous situation. Maybe you don't want to embarrass the person, so you become entangled in a long elaborate lie to save the face of someone you don't even know. A tourist with his family stopped me in the hallway at CBS-TV recently and said, "I've been telling the folks how you and I went to school together in Moosejaw, Canada. I'll bet you'll never forget our English teacher, Mrs. Wilson, will you?" Obviously this man had read that I was born in his home town of Moosejaw, but he didn't know that I never went to school there because I grew up in San Diego, California. I didn't want to face the man down in front of his family, so I just smiled and nodded in agreement—but he didn't let me get away with *that*. He said, "Now tell them about the time Mrs. Wilson kept you after school." So there I stood, making up a story that he knew and I knew was completely false. It was an absolutely ridiculous situation, but his family went away happy.

Sometimes the urge to impress somebody can be downright dangerous. Charlie Correll, who played "Amos" of "Amos 'n' Andy" for years, wanted to show off his piloting skill to his new bride on their honeymoon. He'd flown for years, but he was so excited about his new marriage that he forgot his usual caution and ran out of gas over downtown Los Angeles. As he was spiraling down helplessly, he saw a plane rising from a tiny private airport that he had never known existed. That airport saved their lives. As Charlie said later, "There's nothing more embarrassing than taking your bride up to say, 'Look, no hands,' and she replies, 'Look, no gas.'"

One of the first things a brand-new ensign did after winning his commission in the Navy was to go sailing with his girl friend in her sailboat. He was strictly a powerboat man—didn't know a binnacle from a barnacle—but he took over like an old salt to impress her, and promptly capsized the craft. Then *she* took command, barking orders to get the boat upright again, and sailed him back to the harbor in utter humiliation, with his brand-new officer's cap lost over the side and his uniform wringing wet.

Another newcomer to the rapidly growing group of American boatmen was very proud of his new cabin cruiser and decided to invite half a dozen friends along for its maiden voyage. A crane hoist had barely lowered the craft into the water when it began to sink. Fortunately for the new skipper, one of his guests was an old hand who realized what was happening, and replaced the drain plugs that his host hadn't remembered to check before launching. (There's nothing like a missing drain plug to give you that sinking feeling.)

Some people shy away from impressing others, like former

Sheriff Eugene Biscailuz of Los Angeles. Gene had been given a diamond-studded badge as a symbol of his exalted office, but he was a very informal fellow, and the badge was rather showy, so he always wore it concealed underneath his lapel. One day as he was driving to his office, a rookie deputy of his pulled him over and inquired, none too politely, "Who do you think you are?" Somewhat annoyed that the rookie didn't recognize his own boss, the sheriff said, "That's who I am!"—and pulled back his lapel to flash the diamond badge. The rookie still didn't react— but the sheriff did, when he glanced down and saw that he had left the badge on his other suit.

Another gesture-maker was a nationally known author who generously offered to waive his fee and return his check to a club committee in a small town, after he'd told the audience some of his best stories. The committee members looked at each other, unable to decide whether to accept his gesture, and then excused themselves for a private conference. Returning to the author, they said they would accept his offer and "put it in a special fund." "What's the fund for?" asked the lecturer. The group spokesman shuffled his feet, looked at the floor, and confessed, "It's to get better speakers."

Sometimes it isn't what you say or do that creates an embarrassing scene but how the onlookers interpret it. A lady from my home town of San Diego, California, told me of the day she was walking past an alley with her fiancé. A large rat ran out and she jumped in fright, catching her heel in her fiancé's cuff and tripping him. He fell—and she fell right on top of him. A man ahead of them heard the commotion and turned around. She looked up and said, "A rat." The fellow ahead nodded and said, "He sure is!"

One of life's spicier conversations took place some years ago in eastern Oregon when a new schoolteacher went to a local dance. She was a little overdressed and after a few exhausting whirls around the floor she sat down. A man sitting next to her noticed her fancy clothes and made a fatal guess about her profession. "You must be the new girl," he said. "I've been here about three weeks," she admitted. "How come I haven't seen you around?" said the man. "This is the first time I've been out," she explained. "They sure must be keeping you busy," said he. "Yes," she said,

"I'm just starting and have a lot to learn." "I'd be glad to help," he volunteered. "You hardly seem the type," she said. "You'd be surprised," was his answer. "You're so rugged," she said, "I'd never dream that you ever taught school." The man looked at her in shock and said, "What? Are you a schoolteacher?" She nodded and he backed away in considerable confusion.

More respectable but certainly undignified was the experience of a wedding guest who was late. She was hurrying up the church stairs and came through the door just as the minister was saying the traditional words, "If anyone knows just cause why this couple shall not be married, let them speak now or forever hold their peace." At this moment there was of course a hush—just as she caught her toe in the carpet, fell flat on her face, and yelled involuntarily, "Damn it!"

Some awkward moments are just plain silly, like the experience of a man who built a beautiful doghouse in his basement for his Great Dane and then found it was much too large to get it outside. Or the seventy-five-year-old lady who entered a contest and won a prize—"an anticipation outfit."

One of my favorite sillies involves a woman who went to an optometrist for glasses shortly after her second marriage. The receptionist said the glasses would be mailed to her, and asked for her name and address—but the new bride couldn't remember her new name and had to ask her sister-in-law, "Who am I?"

Here's another silly—a lady wearing a fox fur at a lunch counter heard the man next to her complain, "What happened to my coffee? I had a cup full a minute ago, and it's gone." She glanced down and saw that her fox fur had

dipped into his cup and soaked up every last drop of his coffee.

Another woman told me of the day she weighed herself on a penny scale. "It was broken," she said, "and the needle only went as far as fifty-six pounds—although I weighed about two hundred. A man standing next to me looked at the pointer and said, 'Good God! She must be hollow!'"

A Minneapolis woman remembers her college days when it was a tradition to steal a sorority's trophy whenever you could. One night the girls saw a man running from their sorority with a shiny metal object in his hand. "The trophy!" yelled one of the girls, and the chase was on. The girls not only caught up with the older man—they tackled him. Then they learned the "trophy" was a fire extinguisher that he'd just borrowed because his car was aflame.

It might surprise the young bikini wearers of today to learn that their mothers once wore suits that were even more revealing—although not by design. One former bathing beauty remembers being in a beauty festival during the thirties at the then terribly popular resort of Venice, California. She was feeling fairly confident, even though she was wearing last season's suit, until the judges said, "Turn around please," so they could see her in the round. And see her they did, especially where she hadn't been seen while sitting down waiting for her chance to parade. It seems that she had forgotten after last season to pack mothballs away with her woolen suit, and the moths had redesigned the posterior. When the girl realized what was wrong, she ran offstage without even waving good-by. She couldn't. She didn't have a free hand.

Swimsuit manufacturers today are ingenious engineers and fabric experts, but there were no such designers back in the days when a young lady bought a beautiful all-white suit to go bathing in Cedar Lake, Indiana. It was a very fetching outfit. In fact, as soon as she came up out of the water, the suit fetched a crowd. She hadn't been aware of it, since she had never worn the suit before—but the moment the suit got wet, it also became totally transparent.

A woman who went for a cooling dip in mid-July in the Missouri River was having a wonderful time floating downstream. Then she swung about to go upstream—and felt the current rip away the top of her suit. Frantically she swam downstream again, diving for her bra, but no luck. She had to come out topless. (Ever since I heard that one, I can't stop thinking of that river as the "bra'd" Missouri.)

You're never too old to be embarrassed, as a Fort Lauderdale spinster discovered when she had to have minor surgery and was given the only room available—in the maternity ward.

"You can't imagine how it is to be an old maid in a maternity ward," she told me, "trying to explain why you are in there and having people ask you, 'Which baby is yours?'" To make things even more confusing, a young nurse on night duty was unaware the ward had any occupants except genuine mothers. So when a lady friend of the spinster's called up, the caller was quite shocked to be told, "You can't talk to her right now. It's nursing time and she's feeding her baby."

It was a father-to-be who told me about pacing the floor at a maternity hospital and how delighted he was when a nurse came out and said, "Congratulations. You've just had an eight-pound son; you can come see your wife now." She led him into the darkened room, and he bent down to kiss the new mother just as she yelled, "Nurse! This isn't my husband!" The new "dad" took a closer look. She was right! Back he went to pacing the floor, having already logged two hours waiting for another man's wife, and it took another four hours before his own child arrived—a girl.

A registered nurse told me this one:

"While I was in training, we were learning to give injections. So my roommate had my hip entirely exposed when thirty-five Methodist ministers entered on their tour of the new building."

Now let's leave the hospital scene and go on a romantic ride in one of those old-fashioned amusement park tunnels of love with a Cleveland lady. She was having a wonderful time riding along with her boy friend until the electric power went off. It was quite frightening, being in the pitch darkness, so she insisted that her sweetheart paddle them toward a small window that she could see in the distance. Since she was only five feet tall and weighed ninety pounds, she was able to wriggle her way through the window. Moments later, the lights came on—her eyes adjusted to the glare—and she found herself in the middle of a comfort station filled with men!

Women are supposed to be the blushing sex, but put a man in a compromising situation and he will color up as quickly as any maiden's cheek.

Listen to what happened to a gentleman in Wood Dale, Illinois. He says, "A lady kept eying me in a crowded supermart; then she finally stepped up to me in the checkout line and asked, 'Aren't you the father of one of my children?' Red-faced, I replied, 'Definitely not!' I learned later that she was one of my son's schoolteachers. Oh boy!"

There's obviously no end to the variety of embarrassing situations, yet they all have one thing in common—the unexpected. Embarrassment is always a sneaky punch, landed before we see it coming. We're down for the count before we know what hit us; and while we're lying there, tasting the canvas, we're reminded that life isn't all that dignified.

Just ahead in the next chapter are some zany true stories of automobiles and their drivers, embarrassing moments that could happen only in America, the land of the freeway and home of the brave pedestrian. So fasten your seat belt and let's go!

8

Highway Hangups

We Americans practically live in our automobiles, and if traffic gets much worse, we probably will. The family car is so much a part of our way of life that our activities center around who gets the keys to go where. Comedian Pat Buttram once summed up the situation by saying, "I'm tired of fighting with my son over the car. Next time I want it, I'm going to take it!" Much of our humor has grown up around autos and their drivers—especially women drivers. Now I'm not against women drivers. I would be the last to stand in their way. But it is a fact that all a comedian has to say is that magic phrase "woman driver" and he's off to an evening of laughs. Take Dave Barry, for example, who always scores with this line: "I just bought my wife a second car—a tow truck."

Are women really the scatterbrained fender-benders that men claim? Of course not. And yet it might be fun to explore some true stories that have reddened the cheeks of their heroines.

A lady whose husband had just bought a new car persuaded him to let her try it out while he drove off to work in the old clunker they were keeping for her. She glided around town with the utmost care, as all new car owners do, until it was time to meet her husband downtown for lunch. As she pulled into his office parking lot, her foot missed the brake pedal and there was a heart-rending crunch of metal. She crawled out, gloomily surveying the accordion pleats in her fender, and said to the parking attendant, "How on earth will I ever tell my husband about this?" Then she took a good look at the car she had smashed into. It was the old clunker.

A police officer's wife who was anxious to get home and fix dinner for the children borrowed his car—an unmarked, inconspicuous black sedan. Everything was fine until the engine stalled at a stoplight, right in the middle of rush-hour traffic. Just as she reached for the starter button, traffic screeched to a halt in all directions. Everyone, including her, began waiting for some kind of emergency vehicle, an ambulance or a fire truck, to go by. Then she realized the siren was coming from *her* car. The "starter" she was pressing was the siren button.

A Hollywood housewife told me of the day she made a wrong turn and ended up in line at an automatic car wash. Before she could back out, several other cars pulled in behind her. Resigned to her fate, she watched the car she had washed the day before go down the line, being sprayed and scrubbed.

Another woman had just gotten her driver's license when she heard sirens and pulled over like a good citizen to the side of the road. Seconds later a fireman was pounding on her window, because she had stopped smack in the middle of the fire-station driveway—blocking the fire engine that was sounding the siren.

If you think you were nervous when you took your own

driving examination, think how shaky the license examiners themselves must get when they encounter first-time drivers. A woman in San Francisco confessed to me that when she took her test, her examiner got so nervous that he made her *walk* back to the license bureau. Another young lady went to get her license—and ran into a new car. She didn't get the license, because the man sitting inside the new car happened to be the driving examiner.

A woman who had received a speeding ticket was on

her way to pay it during a brief lunch hour. Then she noticed the blinking red lights in her rear-view mirror, pulled over, and got *another* ticket for speeding.

En route to California from New York, a woman got as far as Gallup, New Mexico. She thought she was on the highway until a man in uniform asked her to park right where she was. Then she discovered she was in a parking lot for a rodeo.

No comedian could top the real-life experience of a man who told me of stopping at a red light and then being rammed by a woman behind him. As they both got out, he told her, "You didn't even slow down. Is there something wrong with your brakes?" "Yes," she confessed, "my husband told me to make sure I pumped up the brakes, and I did. I pumped them up good before I left home."

I can't vouch for this story personally, but I can just see it happening—and maybe it did. A man whose car stalled flagged down a woman motorist and asked if she would give him a push to help get his car going again. "I'd be glad to," she said, "but I don't know how." "It's easy," the man said. "I'll check our bumpers, and if they fit, we'll try it." The bumpers matched, so he told her, "Just get me going in a straight line, and the car should start at around thirty miles an hour." The woman nodded, climbed into her car, and began backing up. Too late the man realized she had misunderstood him. She backed up at least half a block and then began roaring straight at him. As he said later after the crash, "Have you ever watched a car coming at you at thirty miles an hour?"

A lady who couldn't get the family car started told me she called on a neighbor to give her a hand. The neighbor said, "I'll tow you, and if that doesn't start her up, I'll take

you down to the garage." That seemed like a good idea
to her, so he came over, backed up his car, and attached a
towline to her bumper. Everything went smoothly, except
that the engine refused to turn over. Imagine the reaction
of the gas-station attendant, the neighbor, and the woman
when they all looked under the hood and found that there

was no battery. "Lady," said the scornful service-station attendant, "you can't drive a car without a battery." Terribly embarrassed and thoroughly baffled, she telephoned her husband's office. "Oh, I forgot to mention it, honey," he said. "The car wouldn't start this morning, so I took the battery out to get it charged."

Now that we have hammered out a few dents in the records of women drivers, it seems only fair to admit that we men are often automaniacs. Like most drivers, I sometimes zig when I should zag, and I get the outraged glare and the lip-lashing from my next-door driver. But I'm luckier than most, I guess, because instead of a good poke in the eye, I get a front row seat at a fascinating little drama. As the other driver looks at me and his rage begins to abate a little, the first astounded glimmer of recognition appears in his eyes. Then this is gradually replaced by raised eyebrows, a release of the snarling cheek muscles, then a wave of the hand, followed by a warm smile of friendship. The transformation from ogre to cherub is complete in one thirty-second encounter on the freeway!

Inexperienced or unwary tourists are constantly being caught in the maze of new freeways, expressways, and thruways. A traveler from Oregon tells this one on himself:

"I went to New York to see the Yankees play. After spending two hours following directions, I ended up in the Polo Grounds, watching the Bureau of Police playing the Bureau of Sanitation for the championship of New York City."

A teen-age Virginia girl recalls what happened to her dad:

"My father was driving and came to a police road block. The officers didn't stop him, but he was so curious about what they were looking for that he kept driving back through again until they finally did stop him. He found out they were checking drivers' licenses—and his had expired!"

Back in the days when Bob Crane of "Hogan's Heroes" was a disc jockey in Connecticut, he found it handy, he says, to carry a card in his wallet identifying him as a radio personality. Officers who saw it would show him certain courtesies, such as not giving him a ticket. So when Bob came to California, the first thing he did was scribble a little note on the back of his new California driver's license, where any officer would see it. The note said simply, "I am a radio star." (Bob was then doing a very popular disc-jockey show in Los Angeles.)

One day Bob was a little late to the studio, flying along on the freeway, when a motorcycle officer waved him over. The officer asked for Bob's identification, and Bob handed over his new license. The officer examined it without comment, walked to the rear of the car, and began writing down Bob's license-plate number. Then the officer strolled back, smiled politely, and handed Bob a ticket. Across the top of it was written, "I am a policeman."

9

The Name Game

If there is one mistake that is sure to embarrass you, it is forgetting somebody's name. Perhaps you are turning to introduce a person you have known for years, and your mind goes completely blank. You stammer, mumble, kick the rug with your toe, and then confess in misery that the name has somehow escaped you. This fear of forgetting a name is one of the great hazards in show business, because there is no feeling as bad as flubbing the introduction of some international star whose name is everywhere except on the tip of your tongue.

I'll never forget the night I was asked to join a glittering array of celebrities for a movie premiere and a nightclub supper that followed. I was at an enormous table when a distinguished gentleman came up and said, "Hello, Art." I promptly took him around the table and said, "Ladies and gentlemen, this is Noel Coward." Actually I had made a ridiculous error, because he was the great songwriter Cole Porter. But since I had launched upon his introduction so loudly, he was gracious and kind enough to let me proceed without correcting me. When I was tipped off later that I'd confused Cole with Noel, I felt like literally crawling beneath

the table. Fortunately I am still known in the public mind
as something of a jokester, thanks to the gags and stunts
we used to play upon eager volunteers on my "People Are
Funny" show. Occasionally I will make a terrible faux pas
at a party—and the guests will just laugh, saying, "Come on,
Art—you're just kidding."

One time I nearly did myself in both socially and finan-
cially with an advertiser who spent millions in television. I
had only met him once or twice before he came up to me at
a large New York party to say hello. His face was familiar,
but I didn't have the faintest notion who he was. He did
have the sponsorish look of a man who hires you, however,
and with that clue I took a blind guess. "You're . . . ah,
don't tell me, you're . . ." and named the president of the
company that was his biggest competitor! Instead of getting
mad, he burst out laughing and said, "Art, you idiot, you
just never stop ribbing people, do you?"

I still cringe when I think of the night I took my fiancée,
Lois Foerster, to see me announcing on one of my first
coast-to-coast radio shows. It originated at the Mission Beach
Ballroom in San Diego, and the orchestra leader was the
great Freddie Martin himself. Even being near him, I was so
impressed that I could hardly stand it. The thought of introducing him on the air to the whole country was suffocating.
On this night I brought Lois backstage before air time to
introduce her to the great man, to let her see that I actually
knew him and could speak to him. As we approached I
said, "Freddie Martin, I want you to meet . . ." and then
it happened. No name presented itself upon the far horizons
of my unconscious mind. In fact, even Lois's face looked
unfamiliar. Rather than admit to the great Freddie Martin
that I couldn't remember my own fiancée, I blurted out,

"Freddie, this is a young lady who would like to meet you. I can't remember her name because I just picked her up here at the ballroom." It is a great tribute to Lois that our marriage ever took place.

I've had some funny and rather embarrassing moments in the audience while looking for odd and interesting names. I often say to the studio visitors, "If you have an odd name, put up your hand." The other day a woman answered, "My name is Mrs. Sniff." I said, "That is a funny name, Mrs. Sniff." The woman next to her practically broke into hysterics laughing and I said, "Are you with her?" "No," she choked, "but wait until you hear my name." I said, "What is it?" and she said, "Mrs. Smell."

Some people get so excited when I confront them with a microphone that they actually can't answer me when I say, "What's your name?" They can't remember who they are. But what is even worse happened not long ago. A woman in the audience told me, "My name is Mrs. Daisy Anderson." Then she suddenly stopped and put her hand over her mouth and said, "Oh, my God, that was my first husband. My name now is Mrs. Daisy Brown." Mr. Brown was sitting beside her and gave her one of those looks that could kill— or rather not just kill, but draw and quarter.

Years ago I was doing a stunt on the air involving a volunteer who happened to be a rather substantial businessman from St. Louis. The joke was supposed to go like this: I would say, "For a thousand dollars, we'd like to ask you a question." He would reply, "Fine." Then I'd say, "Do you know who is the President of the United States?" and when he would answer, "Harry Truman," I'd spring the gag, saying, "That's fine. Now here is your question—what is his mother's maiden name?" Everything went according to the script until

I reached the point where I said, "Do you know the name of the President of the United States?" He said, "Why certainly, it's . . . ah . . . it's ah . . . the President of the United States?" I said, "Yes. Who is the President?" He began stammering and flushing. "Well," he said, "of course, as everyone knows, it's a . . ." and he gave up. "Oh," he moaned, "I'll never be able to go back to my home town. I'm the chairman there of the Democratic Party!"

One job I definitely would not like to have is that of a State Department attaché who has to escort important foreign visitors around our country. One of these protocol experts told me what happened recently when he escorted a distinguished group of African leaders into the presence of the top officials of one of our biggest cities. One of the local officials who was to introduce the guests to his fellow legislators had an information sheet before him that plainly stated these visitors were from Nigeria. But for some reason, possibly because he didn't know one end of Africa from the other, this particular official welcomed "Our distinguished visitors from Nairobi," which happens to be the name of the capital city of an entirely different country. The visitors were obviously shocked by this slip, which was comparable to introducing Parisians as Peruvians. Another official realized what had happened and nudged the introducer, who now outdid himself by adding, "or whatever country it is." This was not only like running over the visitors, but backing up and running over them again!

Another victim of the foot-in-mouth syndrome was a West Coast literary agent who was invited to an extremely fashionable party in Manhattan, hosted by a big publisher. As he got off the elevator, he realized he had worn the wrong pants with his coat As he describes it, "Nothing could look more skid row than that—a Goodwill coat and Salvation Army pants." But it was too late to change, so he decided to make the best of it. As he and his wife sat down to dinner with more than two dozen people, he saw that all eyes were on a very voluptuous creature about nineteen years old who was then appearing in a Broadway musical. She had a sculptured body and was wearing a flimsy something-or-other with spaghetti straps. The agent leaned over to his wife and said, "I needn't have been concerned about my pants. That girl came in her slip!" His wife broke up, and the man next to her said, "If it's so funny, I'd like to hear it." So she repeated the remark, and then learned the gentleman she was talking to had brought the girl to the dinner.

In the days before the swift jets took over the trans-atlantic flights, I flew back from Europe one night on an old prop plane with a famous blonde star in the seat next to mine. We both napped a great deal of the time on the long, ten-hour trip. About a month later at a big Hollywood party my wife and I were going through the reception line when I saw my friend the blonde. Without thinking, I said, "Oh, hello there. I haven't seen you since we slept together last month."

Another man told me how he managed to ram his foot in his mouth clear up to his ankle while making photographs of a friend's wedding reception. After he shot a candid picture of the bride's mother, the lady laughed and said, "Oh, I'll look awful. My mouth was open." The photographer shook his head reassuringly and said, "Don't worry, you'll look perfectly natural."

Here are some more "Wish I Hadn't Said Thats":

A young carpenter was working on a construction job with an older man who whistled at every woman that went by. Finally a rather frowsy-looking woman came along and the man whistled again. The young carpenter said, "Boy, you'd whistle at anything." The older man glared and said, "That's my wife."

A girl was dating a fellow she had begun to like very much. As the evening came to an end, he kissed her tenderly, looked into her eyes, and whispered, "I'll give you a ring." The next day the girl dashed around town, telling all her girl friends that she was about to be engaged. Then she learned when he called her that he had merely meant to "give her a ring" on the phone. She felt terribly foolish, she told me, but that didn't end the romance. In fact, she did get her ring—with diamonds—two weeks later.

A Nebraska college girl chosen as a delegate to an annual church conference went along with her minister. One afternoon she was needled by the other delegates, who were mostly men, for being late. Apologizing, she said, "Oh, the minister and I were just so tired that we decided to lie down in our room and rest for a while." Seeing the jaws drop, she realized that they didn't know her minister was a *woman*.

Here are a couple of sillies:

An eager young coed who had just enrolled in a very

distinguished Midwestern university was very flustered to meet one of its most eminent professors as she rounded a corner on campus. "Good Jones, Dr. Morning," she said. But she needn't have worried about her tongue twister, because the professor absently replied, "Good Jones, my dear."

Actor Walter Pidgeon addressed a group of clubwomen, and as he was leaving, I'm told, a rather flustered lady stopped him and said, "Oh, my dear Mr. Privilege! This occasion has certainly been a pigeon!"

Here's another zany scene:

A lady standing outside a bank one day noticed a man in a wheelchair, holding a hat in his lap. Feeling compassion for the poor fellow, she dropped fifty cents in his hat. The man snorted angrily at her and threw the coin on the ground—just as a huge black limousine with a chauffeur at the wheel rolled up to the curb for him.

A Florida man tells this one: "We lived in a town where door-to-door salesmen and peddlers were quite a problem, so my wife and I decided not to answer the door for these people. We made up a special ring for ourselves in case either one of us would forget the house keys. It was one long ring and two short ones. One Saturday afternoon, after my wife had gone shopping, I was taking a shower when I heard her special ring. I strode to the door, naked as a jay bird—but when I opened it, there stood our local Avon lady, her eyes bugging out and her mouth wide open. She took off without a word. Every time she saw me after that, she'd avoid me by crossing the street."

This man didn't tell me whether he and his wife still have a "special ring," but if I lived around his house, I don't think I'd give his doorbell one long ring and two short ones!

I don't get really and truly embarrassed very much any more, because practically everything that could happen to me has already happened in the last thirty-three years in this business. But the other day proved that there's an infinite variety of things that can still happen. I was doing what is now one of my oldest and best-established routines, looking in a lady's purse. I always say that a woman treats her purse the same way she does her house. If you look in a woman's purse, you can tell what her house is going to look like when she doesn't expect visitors. The fun is based on a woman now having to reveal the content of her purse, which

ninety-nine times out of a hundred is a shambles. So it's a
funny embarrassing moment—but not serious . . . it's one
of those funny little things. The second thing about a purse
that's both embarrassing and funny is the unexpected nature
of the contents. Am I going to be bitten by a pair of false
teeth that had been left there? Will I run across a note
that will reveal something funny? Will the wife of a minister who happens to be in my audience have a torn mutuel
ticket from a race track? All these things have happened.

Occasionally there are items in women's purses that you
learn by experience to pass over. Not long ago I had a
woman in her sixties who was carrying a likely-looking purse,
which was fat and a little worn-looking. When I opened it
up, the first thing I saw was a plastic device that looked
very prosthetic to me. I had no idea what it was, but it
had several moving parts and some plungers. The whole
thing looked as if it belonged in a doctor's office, not a
woman's purse, so I decided to duck it on the grounds of
caution. As I poked around in the purse, the woman herself
finally reached in and said, "Aren't you going to ask about
this?" With these words, she held the object up! Now I was
stuck. I had to go on. I said, "I did notice it, but I've never
seen anything like it before and I thought maybe it was
something personal and private." She said, "Well, it's a very
interesting and practical device for a woman, because it's a
breast pump." I was absolutely stunned. I just looked at it,
unable to utter a word. The audience was howling, because
every woman there was laughing at my helpless consternation. When I could find my voice again, the best retort I
could think of was, "Well, no wonder I've never seen one
of these. We always took from the dairy." Even as I was
saying this, the thought crossed my mind that this was a

woman in her sixties; and since she had opened the door to this rather embarrassing moment, I could at least be pardoned for pushing it further ajar with the obvious question: "What are *you* doing with one of these things?" "Oh," she said, "I'm just carrying it for a pregnant friend."

10

"Passports, Please"

Now that jetliners span entire oceans and soar over the very ends of the earth, travel is becoming an all-American hobby. No matter where you go, from the fjords of Norway to the lazy climes of Tahiti, you will find the American tourist in his uniform—sportshirt, sunglasses, and camera. Sometimes the braver ones go native, eating raw fish in Japan and cous-cous in Africa, and drinking fermented cactus juice in Mexico. But no guidebook can prepare you for the traps that lie along your path, waiting to snap shut on your poise and dignity. No trip ever goes according to plan, and as I see it, as a man with a lifelong passion for travel, the tourist has only these choices: he can ignore the local customs and get into trouble, or he can follow the local customs—and get into trouble!

The favorite tourist pastime is called "Let's Speak the Local Language." I know because I've played it, and I'm one of the losers. I remember going into a French bank in a small town with an American friend so we could purchase gas coupons for the long drive back to Paris. As tourists we were entitled to a special price, but it meant filling out many forms and waiting an hour while our stamps were okayed.

Meanwhile I conducted all the conversation in the only language spoken there—*le français*. The clerks seemed genuinely amazed and raised their eyebrows in surprise at what I was saying. I assumed they were astonished by my fluent command of French numbers.

Imagine my consternation when I pulled into a gasoline station, proudly handed the man the ticket I had finally received, heard him laugh and say, "Crazy *Américain*." Then he gave my gas tank one quick squirt and said, *"C'est tout, Monsieur."* ("That's all, Mister.") He had given me exactly what my coupon called for—one pint of gas!

My next appearance in a French farce came when I rented one of those mechanically ingenious Citroen automobiles that has as instrument panel like a jet plane. As I drove along through the countryside with my wife and in-laws, people kept pointing to our wheels. I thought I might have a flat, but didn't feel a thump. Finally all those waving arms and pointing fingers made me distinctly uneasy, so I pulled into a garage to see what was wrong. A mechanic came up, opened my door, reached across my lap, pushed a button, and whoosh! The entire car settled down about two feet! It seems before leaving I had pushed a control knob that is used to lift the whole chassis so that the tires can be changed. Meanwhile Lois and her mother had that glassy look that comes from riding a swaying camel. The moral is obvious. When you don't really know your French, don't speak it. Naturally the French have a phrase for it—*Fermez la bouche*.

You might think I would have learned something from my forays into Fractured French, but the urge to speak the native tongue wherever you go is irresistible. When I decided to visit the Orient, therefore, I insisted upon learning some conversational Japanese. After taking several lessons I felt fairly confident that I would not lose face while wagging tongue.

Boarding the plane, I encountered a lovely Oriental stewardess. This was my chance. "Good morning," I said, in my best Japanese. She smiled and bowed graciously. "Your accent is beautiful," she said, "but I'm Chinese."

I've learned some Russian, too, but I have never had the urge to read it, since the alphabet looks so much like something written upside down on the inside of a window. But I was eager to see the Soviet Union, so I doggedly persisted in many long months of negotiations with the Russian Embassy in Washington before finally receiving permission to film a "People Are Funny" show. In fact, it was touch-and-go whether I would leave at all, because I couldn't seem to get that Russian clearance. Just a day or so before I was to leave, my passport finally arrived with the Russian stamp on it, and we caught the next plane for Helsinki, Finland. On arrival in the Finnish capital, we went to the ticket counter to transfer to a Russian plane bound for Leningrad. I handed over our tickets . . . and was told by the clerk that the big black Russian stamp on our visa translated to one word—canceled!

Just going through customs can become quite an adventure, especially if you're trying to play games with the officials. The wife of a prominent advertising man that I know thought it might be fun to smuggle a watch through customs. It wasn't a valuable watch. She just wanted the thrill of being able to sneak something into the country and then brag that nobody had found it. She hid the watch where no official eyes should be prying, in her brassiere. When the plane landed in New York City, she was thunderstruck to learn that all passengers were being searched. The customs agents had a hot tip that one of the passengers was a dope smuggler. Everyone was lined up and being searched minutely, down to the seams and linings of their clothes. As she stood there waiting her turn, she began to perspire profusely in

sheer panic. The smuggler was finally found—standing directly ahead of her in the line—but by then the watch was ruined, drowned by the rivulets of perspiration that ran into it.

Another character I know had a package of dried sunflower seeds with him when he tried to enter Japan. The official informed him that no seeds of any kind could be brought into the country. With a laugh to his friends and a remark that he had paid for them and would bring them in anyhow, my friend opened the sack and gulped down the seeds. He gulped again and his smile vanished when the polite, bowing customs man said he would now have to wait in the station a suitable length of time so that everyone could be sure the seeds did not go into the country. And wait he did.

At the opposite end of the world in Australia, the wife of an American friend with a "station" or ranch next to mine in the Outback decided to bring a baby kangaroo back to the United States. The tiny creature snuggled down in her handbag as happily as though it were in its own mother's pouch, and behaved throughout the entire trip. When the woman arrived in America, the customs official asked if she had anything in her bag to declare. She laughed and said, "Nothing but a live kangaroo." He laughed, too, and said, "Very funny." A few moments later, while waiting for her baggage, she took the baby kangaroo out of the purse for a stroll. As she passed the window of the immigration office, she saw the face of her customs man, stricken and unbelieving.

When in Rome, most Americans seem to enjoy doing what the Romans do. Besides, we do it here at home. But when in Japan, the average American is less than prepared for such local customs as the community bath. One lady vacationing there told me of ending up in a community bath after going through the wrong door. She didn't mind that so much, but everyone else enjoying their afternoon scrub-a-dub was a male Japanese!

One of our Air Force generals told me of being invited to a Japanese general's home. This was a high privilege, so he resolved to follow scrupulously all of the family customs. His first shock came when he was invited to join the family bath, with mama-san, papa-san, and a lovely teen-age daughter. As they all sat there in naked togetherness, the American bravely kept his poise and even attempted conversation with the pretty young miss beside him. "I hope," he said, "to sit next to you at dinner as well." The girl giggled shyly. "I am not allowed to have dinner with honorable visitor," she said. "I do not know you well enough."

It was in the Middle East that a writer friend of mine, Jim Bacon, got into trouble the moment he opened his mouth at the Tel-Aviv airport in Israel. The girl checking passports asked, "What is your name?" "Jim Bacon," he said. "Is Bacon your right name?" said the girl. "Yes." "Sorry," she said. "We just don't allow Bacon in Israel." Jim thought she was putting him on, but he doesn't know to this day. All he does know is that she gave him a currency card and let him through—but she never did stamp his passport.

A Canadian gentleman from Montreal tells me he was tremendously impressed by the elegant furnishings of his hotel suite in Paris. While showering he noticed a cord dangling from the wall and gave it a tug. Almost immediately a lovely young chambermaid appeared and poked her head into the shower where the astonished Canadian stood, covering himself as best he could. "What is it you want, Monsieur," said the matter-of-fact chambermaid, who had been summoned by the bell chord. "A towel!" stammered the Canadian. "And fast!"

A stewardess on a jetliner told me this one about a little old lady who made her first air trip with her. The lady went into the plane's rest room and then stuck her head out and said, "Young lady, do you have any safety pins?" The stewardess supplied some. Later on the lady came out, nodded pleasantly, and the stewardess became curious. What had the woman done with those safety pins? So the stewardess went into the rest room—and there she saw the lady had taken two towels and pinned them together so they would cover the porthole window. Here this lady was afraid somebody might peek in while she was flying at six hundred miles an hour at twenty-seven thousand feet!—obviously a new high in modesty.

Airliners are far safer than the family car for traveling, but inexperienced travelers often carry a cargo of butterflies on their first trip. So you can picture the feeling of a first-timer when his pilot came back into the passenger compartment to retrieve his jacket and overnight bag. As the pilot was buttoning his jacket, the passenger looked nervously up at him and said, "Where are you going?"

You don't have to go flying to foreign lands for travel surprises. You can find plenty right here in the U.S.A. One couple on vacation had their pet Chihuahua along, they told me, and were becoming discouraged because it was getting dark and stormy, and they couldn't find a place to stay where pets were allowed. Finally the woman told her husband, "You go in this place and *don't* mention the dog." A few moments later he waved to her that all was well. She wrapped the dog in a huge pink beach towel, covered his head, and carried him in like a baby. Several guests

were sitting on the porch as she passed. One woman smiled and asked, "Is it a girl?" "Yes," she said. "My only child." The woman reached up, pulled down the blanket for a peek at baby—and the dog barked. "Oh, the little devil has laryngitis again," said the "mother"—and dashed for her room.

A woman riding on a train in a sleeping car shared her

seat with a strange gentleman. At breakfast in a crowded diner the next morning, her four-year-old daughter loudly asked, "Mommy, what's the name of that strange man that you sleep with?"

Another woman told me of her adventures while driving through Arizona. She stopped en route at what she thought would be a suitable hotel. She entered the office and asked the proprietor, "Do you have any vacancies?" "Yes," he said, "but not what you are looking for. This is a mortuary."

A California lady was taking some of her Eastern relatives for a tour of Knott's Berry Farm. Pointing to a cluster of buildings, she said, "These are replicas of the early missions which were established by Father Serra and his followers in the earliest days of California." The visitors were properly impressed, until they noticed there was a certain pattern to the groups of people drifting in and out of these "missions," which were actually rest rooms for the señors and señoras.

It was at Disneyland that a lady, looking through Injun Joe's cave, was admiring the lifelike figure of an enormous cowboy. She turned and patted him playfully on the tummy and said, "How are you doin', pardner?" She nearly fainted when the figure answered, "Fine, lady—but how am I going to explain you to my wife?"

Curiosity was the undoing of a North Carolina woman in her fifties who was on a trip with her family and stopped for dinner in Denver, Colorado. It was a very beautiful restaurant, she told me, and when she went into the ladies' room, she saw a carved statue of a nude man in a fig leaf standing by the commode. Above the statue was this inscription: "Caution. Do not touch fig leaf." Unable to resist, she slowly raised her finger and flipped the fig leaf. It swung to one side—and an alarm bell went off that could be heard

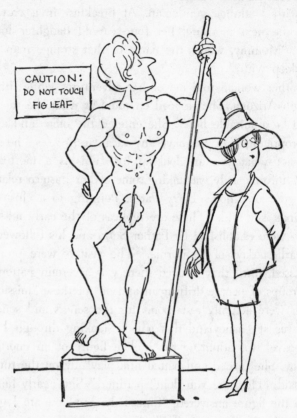

CAUTION:
DO NOT TOUCH
FIG LEAF

a city block. Realizing she'd been trapped in a practical joke, she looked for another exit, but there wasn't even a window to crawl through. Finally she got up enough nerve to open the door, and walked into a crowd of diners who were all in on the gag. The waitress was also shaking with laughter. "Am I the only woman who ever rang the bell?" she asked. "Oh no, dear," said the waitress. "Much older ones than you."

Now we have traveled to the end of this book, and I

hope you've had as much fun as I have along the way. If you saw yourself somewhere in these pages, I'm not surprised. Blushes and bloopers, like history, have a way of repeating themselves. This isn't the kind of book that has a moral, but it does have a message—that people are funny. And I, for one, am glad of it. Aren't you?